T0321583

Learning-Based Local Visual Representation and Indexing

Learning-Based Local Visual Representation and Indexing

By

Rongrong Ji
Yue Gao
Ling-Yu Duan
Hongxun Yao
Qionghai Dai

Amsterdam • Boston • Heidelberg • London • New York • Oxford
ELSEVIER Paris • San Diego • San Francisco • Singapore • Sydney • Tokyo

Executive Editor: Steve Elliot
Editorial Project Manager: Lindsay Lawrence
Project Manager: Anusha Sambamoorthy
Designer: Matthew Limbert

Elsevier
Radarweg 29, PO Box 211, 1000 AE Amsterdam, Netherlands
225 Wyman Street, Waltham, MA 02451, USA
The Boulevard, Langford Lane, Kidlington, Oxford OX5 1GB, UK

Library of Congress Cataloging-in-Publication Data
A catalog record for this book is available from the Library of Congress

British Library Cataloguing in Publication Data
A catalogue record for this book is available from the British Library

ISBN: 978-0-12-802409-6

For information on all Elsevier publications
visit our website at store.elsevier.com

This book has been manufactured using Print On Demand technology. Each copy is produced to order and is limited to black ink. The online version of this book will show color figures where appropriate.

Working together
to grow libraries in
developing countries

www.elsevier.com • www.bookaid.org

CONTENTS

The visual local representation model based on local features and visual vocabulary serves as a fundamental component in many existing computer vision systems. It has widespread application in the fields of object recognition, scene matching, multimedia content search and analysis, and also is the ad hoc focus of current computer vision and multimedia analysis research. The pipeline of the visual local representation model is to first extract the local interest points from images, then quantize such points into visual vocabulary, which forms a quantization table to obtain the feature-space division into visual words. Subsequently, each image is represented as a bag-of-visual-words descriptor, and is inverted indexed into all its corresponding visual words. Research on current computer vision systems have shown that local visual representation models have sufficient robustness against scale and affine transforms and are good at handling partial object occlusion and matching.

However, recent research has also discovered that there are problems in the state-of-the-art visual local representation models, i.e., insufficient visual content discriminability, extreme dense representation, as well as an inability to reveal higher-level semantics. This book focuses on the study of local feature extraction, quantization errors and semantic discriminability in visual vocabulary, as well as the visual quantization errors, semantic discriminability during the visual vocabulary construction, and the visual phrase based visual vocabulary representation problem.

In the local feature extraction, both spatial and category contexts are exploited, which puts forward the interest-point detection from a local scope toward a global scope. In the unsupervised learning of visual vocabulary and its indexing, the quantization errors in the traditional visual vocabulary are investigated, which further reveals the difference between visual words and textual words, and the influence of narrowing this difference. In the supervised learning of visual vocabulary and its indexing, the image labels are introduced to supervise the visual vocabulary construction, which achieves learning-based quantization in local feature space. Finally, based on the optimized visual vocabulary model, the extension from visual words to visual phrases is investigated, together with its usage and combination manners with the traditional bag-of-visual-words representation. The main contents of this book are as follows.

In the stage of interest-point detection, a context-aware semi-local interest-point detector is proposed. This detector integrates maximum outputs in image scale space with spatial correlations for interest-point detection. First, the multiple-scale spatial correlations of local features are integrated into a difference of contextual Gaussian (DoCG) field. Experiments have revealed that it can fit the global saliency analysis results to a certain degree. Second, the mean shift algorithm is adopted to locate the detection results within the difference of contextual Gaussian field, in which the training labels are also integrated into the mean shift kernels to enable the finding of "interest" points for subsequent classifier training.

In the stage of unsupervised learning for constructing visual vocabulary and its indexing, a density-based metric learning is proposed for unsupervised quantization optimization. First, using fine quantization in informative feature space and coarse quantization in uninformative feature space, the quantization errors in visual vocabulary construction are minimized, which produces more similar distribution from visual words to textual words. Second, a boosting chain-based hierarchical recognition and voting scheme is proposed, which improves the online recognition efficiency while maintaining its effectiveness and discriminability.

In the state of supervised visual vocabulary learning, a semantic embedding-based supervised quantization approach is proposed. This approach introduces the image labels from the web to build the semantic sensitive visual vocabulary. First, a feature-space density-diversity estimation algorithm is introduced to propagate the image labels from image level into local feature level. Second, the supervised visual vocabulary construction is modeled into a hidden Markov random field, in which the observed field models the local feature set, while the hidden field models the user label supervision. The supervision in the hidden field is achieved via Gibbs distribution over the observed field, and the vocabulary construction is treated as a supervised clustering procedure on the observed field. Meanwhile, we adopt WordNet to model the semantic correlations for user labels in the hidden field, which effectively eliminates the labels synonym.

In the stage of visual vocabulary-based representation, a co-location visual pattern mining algorithm is proposed. This algorithm encodes the spatial co-occurrence and correlative positions of local feature descriptors into co-location transactions and leverages Apriori algorithm to mine the co-location visual patterns. Such a pattern is second order and is sensitive to category information, which serves as more discriminative and lower dimensional local visual descriptions. In addition, such sparse representation, together with the original bag-of-visual-words representation, can further improve the visual search precision in visual search and recognition experiments in benchmark databases, which has been proven in quantitative experimental comparisons.

LIST OF FIGURES

LIST OF TABLES

LIST OF ALGORITHMS

CHAPTER 1

Introduction

1.1 BACKGROUND AND SIGNIFICANCE

Computerized visual representation aims to leverage computer analysis techniques to allow machines to "see" the environment, such that the appearances and structures of physical scenes can be obtained. In this scenario, discriminative information representations (visual features) are extracted for the subsequent visual inference and recognition tasks. The main intelligence of computer vision lies in its ability to obtain the informative "knowledge" from images or videos, which is further used to make "decisions" as in traditional artificial intelligence systems. It simulates the key functionality of human visual systems. The human visual system is widely acknowledged as one of the most powerful biological vision systems, with the ability to not only passively receive information, but also actively "sense" information. The computerized simulation of the human visual system has a long story such as visual content receiving, interpretation, and response to visual stimulus, with help from fields such as signal processing, machine learning, and pattern recognition.

The main trend of current visual search and matching techniques lies in the visual dictionary model, which is built based on local feature representations. Compared to traditional global feature representation, local feature representation has been demonstrated to be more robust in terms of photographing variances in image viewing angles, lightings, scale changes, etc. On the other hand, as a result of the large success of document retrieval, models such as bag-of-words or hashing have been introduced to generate image signatures. These efficient and effective image representations are widely used in image search, object recognition, and multimedia event-detection systems. For example, bag-of-words is used to quantize the local features extracted from images into corresponding frequency histograms of visual words. On this basis, traditional techniques in documentation retrieval (like TF-IDF, pLSI, and LDA) can be directly applied to improve multimedia search and recognition performance.

Visual content representation is the core problem in multimedia analysis, retrieval, and computer vision research. During the last decade, the major research focus in visual content representation has switched from global and regional features to local features that are extracted from local image blobs or corners. Serving as the basis of visual content representation, the idea of extracting and describing local features was inspired by the study of motion tracking and analysis. For instance, Hannah et al. proposed the first algorithm for corner detection in images [1]. Subsequently, Harris et al. adopted the ratios of eigenvalues of the second-order matrix of the surrounding region to detect and describe interest points [2]. Upon this basis, different corner detectors were proposed [3–5]. Recently, more theoretical analysis and formulations about corner detector have been given in [6]. To cope with the demand for invariances of small image regions in rotations, scales, and affine transforms, Schmid et al. [7] proposed the Hessian affine local feature detector. Among them, one of the most representative methods is the SIFT (Scale-Invariant Feature Transform) proposed by D. G. Lowe, [8, 9] which handles the invariances of scale and partial affine transform from the perspective of scale space theory. A detailed review of related work in local feature detectors up to 2005 can be found at [10]. Another origin of local feature comes from the inspiration of biological research. The biological vision system serves as a natural local visual system. For instance, Hubel and Wiesel have discovered that the visual receptive field is a natural local feature detector and processor [11]. Marr proposed to summarize low-level image processing problems as a sort of local feature extraction, which includes extracting edge, bar, blob and terminator [12]. Zhu and Poggio et al. have shown that, based on such local feature extractions, almost all information for each individual image can be represented based upon image-edge features [13, 14].

A subsequent problem after local feature extraction is how to describe these local features in an effective and efficient manner. The current methods used either visual dictionary or hashing techniques with inverted file indexing to overcome the matching deficiency between two sets of local features. Furthermore, to handle the scalability, the visual dictionary is typically learnt by hierarchical k-means to accelerate both the offline dictionary construction and the online local feature quantization. However, quantization procedures such as k-means would bias the clustering procedures to be concentrated into the densest regions in the local feature space, resulting in discriminability degeneration in the resulting bag-of-visual-words histogram. In addition, for the visual dictionary-based representations, current approaches still output a high-dimensional sparse representation in the bag-of-words histogram, which is indeed less efficient as the content signature. Finally, how to integrate the learning mechanism into different levels of local feature quantization is still unclear; however, this is one of the major functionalities in the learning procedure of human visual systems.

So far, existing works in visual local representation are still based on the visual statistics of local features. Although such representation offers sufficient robustness for traditional visual matching problems, the semantic gap between low-level visual content representation and high-level semantic understanding remains, which has slowed progress in related fields such as visual object detection, recognition, and multimedia content tagging. Such a gap serves as the main bottleneck in existing visual local representation research. In contrast, during the evolution of the human visual system, its corresponding visual representation mechanism has been largely affected and influenced by its environment, in terms of learning its optimal representation strategy to effectively characterize scene contents. In other words, the learning mechanism plays an important role in the feature detection and representation of human vision systems, which indeed is one of the most important reasons the human vision system is able to obtain meaningful visual representation through limited and sparse observations from outer scenes.

This book provides a systematic introduction to how the machine learning mechanism can be used in local feature representation and indexing. By integrating learning components, the goal is to build a more effective and efficient visual local representation to benefit computer vision research. In particular, this book focuses on how machine learning can be used to build the components of local feature detection, quantization, and representation, as well as its scalability to deal with massive data. It begins with learning-based semi-local interest-point detection, connected by unsupervised visual dictionary optimization and supervised visual dictionary learning, and finally builds upon higher-level visual pattern representation. More specifically, this book reviews work in the following perspectives:

- The book first focuses on how to extract a semi-local interest point that is more semantic-aware and with a larger spatial scale to use as the basis of the subsequent visual dictionary construction. To this end, a context-aware semi-local feature detector (CASL) is proposed, which combines (1) the spatial context of nearby local features and (2) the semantic labels of the targeted image to carry out the real "interest"-point detection at a higher level.

- The book then focuses on how to improve the hierarchical local feature quantization procedure from an unsupervised perspective. To this end, a density-based metric learning (DML) is proposed to refine the distance metric distortion during hierarchical k-means based visual dictionary construction.

- Thirdly, improving the visual dictionary from a supervised manner is proposed, which is achieved by exploring the readily available social tags from reference images, based on a proposed generative embedding of supervised tag information. This is achieved by a hidden Markov random field to supervise the dictionary building as well as modeling the tag similarity and correlation.

- Finally, based on the learned optimized dictionary, this book further exploits its potential usage for visual pattern generation, together with its potential to improve the traditional bag-of-visual-words model. To achieve this goal, a gravity-distance based co-location pattern mining approach is proposed to extend the traditional transaction-based co-location pattern mining scheme.

1.2 LITERATURE REVIEW OF THE VISUAL DICTIONARY

The visual dictionary serves as one of the most important and fundamental components in the research of visual local representation. Different from the traditional global features or filter-based features, the visual dictionary can be regarded as a sort of data-driven feature extractor, whose performance therefore highly influences the subsequent bag-of-words representation. From a higher perspective, visual local representation and indexing involve multi-disciplinary research fields including computer vision, pattern recognition, signal processing, information retrieval, machine learning, and cognition science. The visual dictionary together with the local feature extraction serves as a key component in image and video retrieval, scene recognition, object detection, image classification, video surveillance, image matching, three-dimensional reconstruction, as well as robotic navigation.

In the past decade, local features and the visual dictionary have been widely studied in computer vision. For instance, the Visual Computing Group at Oxford University led by A. Zisserman has done a lot of pioneering work in visual dictionary-based image/video search and scene matching.

For example, the Video Google system uses *k*-means clustering to build the visual dictionary together with the inverted indexing structure for large-scale near-duplicate video retrieval. In terms of object recognition, Fei-Fei Li et al. at Princeton and Stanford universities have done quite a lot of work on local feature-based object modeling and scene recognition [15]. To cope with the construction and search deficiency, D. Nister et al. from the Center for Visualization and Virtual Environments at the University of Kentucky have proposed the so-called Vocabulary Tree model [16], which exploits the hierarchical *k*-means clustering-based strategy to build the visual dictionary. For mobile-based location search, the Photo2Search system [17] developed by the Web Search and Mining Group at Microsoft Research Asia is one of the pioneering works.

There has been active research on visual local representation and indexing as reported in academic publications, especially at the competitive peer-review conferences worldwide such as the IEEE International Conference on Computer Vision, IEEE International Conference on Computer Vision and Pattern Recognition, European Conference on Computer Vision, and ACM Multimedia. For example, when searching with the keywords "local feature" in the Proceedings of CVPR 2009, over 100 papers resulted (in total about 250). In addition, there are many related tutorial and workshops at these conferences. Beyond conference proceedings, papers concerning visual local representation and indexing are also well published in major peer-review journals such as the *International Journal of Computer Vision, IEEE Transactions on Pattern Analysis and Machine Intelligence, IEEE Transactions on Image Processing, IEEE Transactions on Multimedia, Pattern Recognition, and Computer Vision and Image Understanding*, with many special issues.

1.2.1 Local Interest-Point Extraction

Local feature detector and descriptor: Generally speaking, obtaining local features from a target image refers to both the detection and description phases. The task of local-feature extraction is to discover and locate the salient regions (or so-called interest points), such as corners or conjunctions within a given image. Such interest points are supposed to have a strong response to a series of filters in either spatial or frequency domains, e.g., difference of Gaussians filters, while their description should be robust to a series of photographing variances such as viewing angle changes, lighting condition changes, rotations, affine transforms, and partial occlusions. There have been many representative interest-point detectors proposed in recent years, such as SIFT [9], PCA-SIFT [18], GLOH [10], Shape Context [19], RIFT [20], MOP [21], and the learning-based MSR descriptor [22, 23]. Among them is the concept of combining the difference of Gaussians-based interest-point detection with SIFT-based interest-point description. As one of the most popular local feature extractor, the SIFT (scale invariant feature transform) [9] descriptor adopts scale–space theory to achieve the invariant description of the local interest point with respect to the scale and rotation changes. In [9], local minimal and maximal in the scale space are first detected, subsequently the detected regions are rotated into its main gradient direction. As described, the corresponding pixel region is subdivided into 4×4 blocks, within each of which an 8-dimensional histogram is extracted, resulting in a 128-dimensional descriptor in total. To further accelerate the extraction and reduce the descriptor size, Ke et al. further proposed to do dimension reduction based on this extracted 128-dimensional vector, resulting in the so-called PCA-SIFT [18]. There is no doubt that the SIFT descriptor and its variances are the most common interest-point descriptors used in the literature, with good invariances to the photographing variances in rotations, scales, and affiance transforms, providing sufficient robustness for matching images captured from different perspectives.

Using the SIFT feature as an example, the local feature extraction and description contains the following two stages: The first stage is the difference of Gaussians or dense sampling based interest-point detection, which includes the following three detailed steps:

1. Scale space construction and local maximal/minimal point detection, to locate the initial locations of interest points and their corresponding scales.
2. Filter out the edge points with a one-directional gradient response, based on Hessian matrix-based operations (the ratio between the matrix trace and determinant).
3. Rotate the region of each interest point, based on its main gradient direction, which ensures the subsequent descriptor is rotation invariant.

The second stage is the aforementioned SIFT descriptor extraction.

1.2.2 Visual-Dictionary Generation and Indexing

Working mechanism of the visual dictionary: Most existing visual dictionaries, such as the vocabulary tree model [16], the approximate k-means clustering [24], the locality sensitive hashing [25], and the hamming embedding [26], are built based upon the quantization of the local feature space, aiming to subdivide the local reference features extracted from the image database into visual word regions. Then, for a given image to be searched or matched, the algorithm extracts a variant number of local features and then uses the learnt visual dictionary to quantize these local features into a bag-of-words histogram. Such a histogram offers good robustness against partial occlusions and further invariances to heavier affine transforms. Another advantage comes from the capability to leverage traditional techniques in document retrieval that have been proven to be very effective in visual search problems, such as TF-IDF, pLSI, and LDA.

Hierarchical structure: With the increasing size of the image/video corpus, there are challenges for the traditional visual search and matching techniques. For instance, the system needs to process a massive amount of visual local features (e.g., there are two to three million SIFT features extracted from 30,000 images). In an online query there is no way to store such massive data in the memory or to do a real-time online search within such a gigantic dataset. Although the traditional k-d tree indexing can process the massive data, it typically fails in handling high-dimensional data such as 128-dimensional SIFT feature space, where the matching efficiency would occasionally degenerate to linear scanning. On the contrary, the visual dictionary adequately addresses these challenges with the principle of (hierarchical) local descriptor quantization with inverted indexing, which ensures the search time cost is unrelated to the scale of the image dataset.

As one of the most representative schemes used to build the visual dictionary, the vocabulary tree (VT) model [16] adopts hierarchical k-means clustering to do quantization definition of "hierarchy" is subdividing a given set of local features into k-clusters at each layer (k is the branching factor, and $k = 3$ in this example), which results in Voronoi region divisions, typically implemented in a recursive manner. To search a large-scale high-dimensional dataset, the vocabulary tree serves as a very effective and efficient model structure. The clustering stops either when the current tree structure has achieved the maximal hierarchical layer, or when the number of local interest points to be clustered is smaller than a given threshold. From the above definition, the vocabulary tree finally outputs a tree structure with depth L and branch k, containing approximately k^L nodes. The finite nodes (without any children) can be regarded as visual words, each of which contains the local features that are closest to this word centroid rather than the other words.

Online query involves comparing each extracted local feature to the visual dictionary to find a more similar visual word. Again, in the case of a hierarchical dictionary structure, this is done by querying the local feature with the centroids in each layer to decide which subtree to go to in the next layer. Finally, when locating the best matched words, images that are inverted indexed in this word are picked up and pushed to a similarity list, where the IDF-based weighting might also help to differentiate the votings of this word.

The data structure of the tree-based quantization can be categorized into two parts: (1) the feature-based partition tree, which is based on subdividing the data in individual dimensions, with subsequent mapping of the data subset to its corresponding subregion (representative approaches include the K-D tree, R-tree, and Ball-tree); and (2) the data-based partition tree (metric tree), which is based on directly subdividing the data within its original feature space, for which there are representative works like k-means, approximated k-means, and hierarchical k-means.

Visual dictionaries commonly exist in current visual search and recognition systems. Their structure plays an important role in the subsequent visual search and recognition performance [16, 27]. The vocabulary tree is a metric tree, where the resulting visual word subdivisions can be visualized as 2-D Voronoi regions.

Similar to the TF-IDF in the document retrieval, each image j can be represented as a vector $d_j = (W_{1j}, \ldots, W_{n_t j})$, in which n_t is the number of visual words in the visual dictionary. Each dimension in this vector is weighted by its term frequency and inverted document frequency (TF-IDF) together to represent its discriminativity (relative importance) to the bag-of-words histogram. The calculation of TF-IDF is:

$$W_{i,j} = W_{i,j}^{tf} \times W_{i,j}^{idf}, \tag{1.1}$$

where the TF (term frequency) [28] reveals the importance of this word in the target image and is obtained by calculating the occurrence frequency of this word in the target image as:

$$W_{i,j}^{tf} = \frac{n_j^i}{n_j}, \tag{1.2}$$

where n_j^i is the time that the ith visual word appears in the jth image and n_j is the total number of visual words appearing in the jth image.

For IDF, intuitively, if a given word appears in too many images, it has little to add to the corresponding image representation. On the contrary, if the word appears in only a few images, it is of great importance to the corresponding image representation. Such importance is opposite to the frequency of this word appearing in different images, which is revealed as IDF (inverted document frequency) [28], as:

$$w_{i,j}^{idf} = \log\left(\frac{N}{n_i}\right), \tag{1.3}$$

where N is the number of images in the data and n_i is the number of images that are inverted indexed in the ith visual word. Based on the aforementioned TF-IDF weights, the image similarity between the two images is the weighted Cosine distance of their corresponding bag-of-words vectors.

Quantization error: The building of a visual dictionary introduces many important issues that influence the subsequent visual search and recognition performances, which is mainly due to the process of quantizing continuous local feature descriptors into discrete subregions in the local descriptor feature space [9, 15, 27, 29, 30]. Nister et al. [16] investigate the combination of multiple layers to build a hierarchical bag-of-words model, which aims to improve the finest quantization errors by embedding its higher-level node similarity. Jurie et al. [31] adopt adaptive distance metrics to improve the mean shift effect in the k-means clustering. Yang et al. [32] investigate the factors of dictionary size, soft quantization strategy, and different pooling methods, IDF weightings, and stop-word removal techniques to the final retrieval and classification performance. There are also existing works that focus on the learning-based visual word selection to build a better bag-of-words histogram representation. For instance, boosting-based codeword selection with mutual information maximization criterion is proposed in [33] and [34]. The bottleneck of such methods lies in the dependency of the training phase as well the ignoring of the middle-level dictionary representation in the dictionary hierarchy. For instance, works in [31] and [35] do not consider the case of hierarchical structure to the final retrieval performance; and work in [32] cannot guarantee the resulting codebook construction is optimal, with a certain random style to build an optimal codebook. Finally, the works in [33] and [10] heavily rely

Figure 1.1 Visualized example of a visual dictionary.

on supervised labels, which therefore prevent their potential extension to large-scale settings (Figure 1.1).

Inspirations from the text domain: In document retrieval, there is not a clear definition of textual word hierarchy. On the contrary, in visual words, especially in the vocabulary tree-based model, the hierarchical structure highly affects the subsequent visual search and recognition performance. During the hierarchical quantization of visual words, not only the finest level of leaf nodes (visual words) but also their middle-level representation are built. In other words, such a hierarchical dictionary structure not only provides the lower-level bag-of-words representation but also their higher-level abstraction. The works in [31] and [36] have shown that the k-means clustering can show bias to the dense regions in the local feature space, called the mean shift effect [37], and therefore the feature-space division is not bias. Furthermore, the hierarchical subdivision can amplify this unbiased mean shift effect, which results in a very unbalanced feature-space division. One significant effect is that, the more discriminative the region (i.e., it appears in fewer images and hence is more sparse) the more coarsely quantized and a low IDF is obtained, while the less discriminative region (i.e., it appears in more images and hence is more dense) would be heavily quantized and a high IDF would be obtained. This book will show that this problem is the exact reason previous works [30, 32] reported that the IDF was not as good as expected. From this point, the book will further propose an unsupervised feature-space quantization scheme to alleviate the above unbalanced feature-space hierarchical subdivision.

Supervised dictionary learning: Despite the branch of works in unsupervised distance metric learning, recently supervised or semi-supervised dictionary optimization has also received increasing research focus. For example, the work in [38] proposed a Markov random field model with must-link and cannot-link to do supervised data clustering. Mairal et al. proposed a sparse coding-based discriminative, supervised visual codebook construction strategy [39], which has been validated in the tasks of visual object recognition. Lazebnik et al. proposed a mutual information minimization-based supervised codebook learning [40], which requires supervised labels on the exact local descriptor level. Moosmann et al. proposed an ERC-Forest model [41] to leverage the descriptor level supervision to guide the indexing tree construction. The works in [42–44] also proposed to subdivide or merge the original codewords learned from the originally unsupervised dictionary construction, so as to build a category (or image)-specific codebook to refine the subsequent classifier training or image search. One of the major limitations of [42–44] lies in the fact that their computation complexity is at least linear to the category number, and are therefore unable to scale up to massive amount of Web images with tens of thousands of semantic labels.

It is worth mentioning that learning-based quantization has also been included in the research of data compression, as in [45–47]. To this end, models such as self-organized map [46] or regress loss minimization model [47] have been adopted to minimize the reconstruction loss between the local features and the quantized codewords. Also, works in [48, 49] proposed to combine the spatial constraint into the clustering of textual regions to produce the texton dictionary. However, the aforementioned works in supervised dictionary learning do not take into account the semantic correlation, and therefore can not handle the label correlations well. However, this is the main limitation if the algorithm need to learn from the Web. In addition, the existing learning-based visual representation [15, 39–44, 50] only considers the case where the supervised labels are on the local feature level rather than the global (image) level, so the learning effectiveness is also limited.

Feature hashing: In addition to the visual dictionary models based on feature-space quantization, the Approximate Nearest Neighbor Search can be also used to handle the large-scale feature matching problem in the high-dimensional feature space. In such a setting, the Locality Sensitive Hashing (LSH) approach and its variants [51–53] has been widely used. LSH is a sort of hashing technique to ensure the neighborhood hashing results are meaningful and represent similarity. Its main idea is to leverage a group of independently calculated hashing functions to project the high-dimensional space into low-dimensional space for search and indexing, such that the finding of the nearest neighborhood can be guaranteed. This property enables a direct comparison of the hashing code to come up with a similarity measurement of the two local features. The recent works have also demonstrated that the Hamming distance can be further used to provide a good approximate of the distance metric [54, 55] when comparing two hashing codes. Moreover, kernel-based similarity metrics are also proposed in [40, 56, 57] and have been shown to have good effectiveness and large acceleration in large-scale visual matching problems.

Multi-tree based indexing: Another technique beyond hashing for fast nearest neighborhood searching is multi-tree based indexing. One of the most well-known examples is the k-d tree and k-d forest, whose main idea is to iteratively find the best dimension in the feature space to subdivide the reference dataset. There are different criteria used to guide the division within individual dimensions, such as maximizing the information gain after division. To further extend this idea, the work in [58] adopts a best bin first (BBF) search strategy to efficiently find the best matching under a given threshold. Other related works include [59–61]. For instance, Nene and Nayar et al. proposed a slicing technique in [62], which adopts a series of two-dimensional binary search techniques to sort data within each dimension to reduce the nearest neighborhood search complicity. Grauman and Darrell et al. in [63] proposed to reweight the matchings at different tree dimensions to further reduce the matching errors. Muja and Lowe et al. [64] proposed to compare not only one dimension each time in the feature tree indexing structure, and improves the randomized k-d tree based visual similarity search.

Visual pattern mining: Due to the ignoring of spatial correlation between different visual words in the reference image, there are many mismatches caused by visual dictionary-based quantization [10, 29, 65]. In recent works [66–68], spatial combinations of visual words (called visual phrases) have been used to replace traditional bag-of-words based non-spatial representations. For instance, the work in [29] proposed a constellation model to model the joint spatial distribution of visual words for a given object category for object classification and detection. However, the constellation model is generative and typically involves adjusting lots of parameters so is unfeasible for handling large-scale data. The work in [65] proposed a middle-level model representation built upon the geometric constellation of visual words to learn different parts of a given object, while the parameter ordering problem in [29] is handled to a certain degree. However, due to the requirement of strong geometric constraint as a prior, the work in [29] cannot be scaled up to the problem of large-scale visual matching.

Following the idea of visual pattern/phase discovery, there are many related works devoted to mining the representative spatial combination of visual words in the recent literature [69–72]. These works [69–72] can be mainly categorized as transaction-based co-location pattern mining, which depends on the modeling of spatial co-location statistics of visual words into transactions. Compared to the previous works that rely on strong prior knowledge, these works [69–72] advance in their unsupervised manner of feature representation.

In [69], Sivic et al. proposed to use viewpoint invariant features to build the initial visual words by k-means clustering, with a frequent item set mining technique to discover the most frequently found spatial combinations of word pairs or subsets. In [70], Quack et al. proposed to discovered the most frequent objects in a given scene in an unsupervised manner, where the candidate objects are detected by mining the frequently appeared spatial combinations of visual words. In [71], Yuan et al. proposed a visual phase mining model and used the mined visual phase to refine the original similarity metric of bag-of-words. The work in [72] further leveraged the mined visual patterns to filter out the initial visual words extracted from dense sampling.

Geometric verification: Beyond visual pattern or phase-based mining, the spatial cues also play an important role in visual search, as the information used to do spatial verification-based post-processing, e.g., the RANSAC [9, 24, 30, 73] operator. However, due to its low efficiency, RANSAC-based methods [9, 24, 30, 73] are typically used to do post-processing. As an alternative, the work in [30, 74] proposed to do a spatial voting of nearby matching pairs for a given local feature, and the bundled-based features are proposed in [75] to further improve the search accuracy.

Visual word correlations: Another direction for visual dictionary post-processing is to analyze the visual words as well as the target images.

For instance, Jing et al. proposed to simulate the visual feature matching between images as hyperlinks between webpages, based on a PageRank-like mechanism [76] to achieve the selection of representative images. In addition, many widely used models in topical analysis in document retrieval, such as latent semantic analysis (LSA), can be further leveraged for extracting middle-level image representation from visual words. LSA needs pre-defined topical numbers, which are used to carry out singular value decomposition (SVD) for the topical feature extraction. Such a fixed-number topical setting is given in [77, 78] by adopting latent topical models like pLSA [77] or latent Dirichlet analysis (LDA) [78].

1.3 CONTENTS OF THIS BOOK

A scale beyond local: The first work introduced in this book is to challenge the independent assumption among the local interest-point detection procedures [8, 29, 79–81]. In the previous setting, each interest point is assumed to be conditional independent, and therefore their detection processes do not influence each other. However, in many multimedia analysis and computer vision tasks, the detected local features are treated as a whole in the subsequent processing. For example, adopting a support vector machine to map the bag-of-words histogram into a high-dimensional space where the separated hyperplane is found. From this perspective, the performance of interest-point detectors not only depends on the detection repetitiveness, but also depends on whether the ensemble of all detected local features are discriminative enough for the subsequent feature mapping or classification. The same conclusion also comes from observations of the human visual system [82], where the V1 cortex in the human brain (which can be simulated as Gabor-like local filter bands) generates a spatial context that is further processed by the V2 cortex [83] by its complex cells, resulting in a so-called semi-local stimulus for the further processing. Therefore, a natural question is: Can we make use of the spatial and semantic context of local descriptors to discover more discriminative "semi-local" interest points?

Unsupervised dictionary optimization: The visual dictionary contains not only the finest-level visual words but also their higher-level abstraction. Therefore, such structural abstraction provides natural cues to improve the search performance by combining the middle-level bag-of-words with the finest-level bag-of-words. However, the study in [16] has found that such a hierarchical weighted (with IDF weights) combination does not achieve significant performance gain as expected. In this book, we further argue that this performance deficiency can be further saved based upon an optimized dictionary hierarchy learned in an unsupervised manner. To this end, a distance-based metric learning (DML) approach is proposed to improve the hierarchical k-means clustering. Consequently, a hierarchical recognition chain is proposed to simulate the coarse-to-fine decision in the Boosting chain classifier [84] for high efficiency retrieval.

Supervised dictionary learning: The existing works concerning the visual dictionary are mainly based on unsupervised local feature-space quantization, based upon the visual contents as introduced in [16, 24–26]. However, some recent works have started to exploit supervised dictionary learning [39–41] and semantic labels, especially the correlative image tags from the Web. Semantic tags are widely used in classifier training tasks. In this book, a supervised dictionary learning scheme is introduced based upon the generative Markov random field, with the help of image tag correlation modeling to achieve a better supervised dictionary learning from imprecise and correlative semantic labels.

This approach aims to address two main challenges in large-scale supervised dictionary learning: (1) How to obtain large-scale precise local feature supervision if only the image (global) supervision is available, when in such a case manual annotation is unfeasible. This is addressed by leveraging the readily available image tags from social media websites such as Flickr and Facebook together with a global-to-local tag propagation scheme; and (2) how to model such correlative and numerous tags, which is achieved by proposing a hidden Markov random field-based generative semantic embedding scheme.

Visual pattern mining: Finally, the book proposes to further mine meaningful visual words into visual patterns, and subsequently study its potential improvement to the traditional bag-of-words based visual search paradigm. We have discovered that the traditional transaction-based co-location pattern mining scheme typically tends to discover texture regions. To handle this problem, a distance-based co-location mining is further proposed. Meanwhile, to better handle the drawback in the traditional Euclidean distance measure in visual pattern mining schemes, a gravity distance is further proposed in the distance-based co-location mining scheme.

CHAPTER 2

Interest-Point Detection: Beyond Local Scale

2.1 INTRODUCTION

In recent years, local interest points, a.k.a., local feature or salient regions, have been widely used in a large variety of computer vision tasks, ranging from object categorization, location recognition, image retrieval, to video analysis and scene reconstruction. Generally speaking, the use of local interest points typically involves two consecutive steps, called the *detector* and *descriptor* steps. The detector step involves discovering and locating areas where interest points reside in a given image, e.g., corners and junctions. Such areas should contain strong signal changes in more than one dimension, and can be repetitively identified among images captured with different viewing angles, cameras, lighting conditions, etc. To provide repeatable and discriminative detection, many local feature detectors have been proposed; for instance, Harris-Affine [80], Hessian-Affine [81], MSER [29], and DoG [8].

The descriptor step involves providing a robust characterization of the detected interest points. The goal of this description, in combination with the previous detection operation, is to provide good invariance to variations in scales, rotations, and (partially) affine image transformations. Over the past decade, various representative interest-point descriptors have also been proposed in the literature; for instance, SIFT [9], GLOH [10], shape context [19], RIFT [20], MOP [21], and learning-based (MSR) descriptors [22, 23].

In this chapter, we will skip the basic concepts of how typical detectors and descriptors work. Instead, we discuss in detail a fundamental issue: the detector scale. Generally speaking, the detector operation provides scale invariance to a certain degree, thanks to the scale space theory. However, our concern here is, whether the detection should be at the scale of the "isolated" interest point, or in a higher scope; for example, by investigating the spatial correlation and concurrence among these *local* interest points. So far, the detector phase of each local feature has been treated in an isolated manner [8, 29, 80, 81]. To this end, each salient region is detected and located separately. We term the proposed detector Context-Aware Semi-Local (CASL) detector.

However, one interesting observation is that, in many computer vision applications, the interest points are proceeded together in the rest recognition or classification steps. In other words, in the rest operations, the recognition or classification system investigates their joint statistics. It is therefore a natural guess that the linking (or middle-level representation) among such "local" interest points would be more important. The inspirations also come from the study of human visual systems [82]. For instance, it has been discovered that the contextual statistics of simple cell responses in the V1 cortex (can be simulated by local filters such as Gabor) are integrated into complex cells in V2 [83] to produce semi-local stimuli in visual representation.

Therefore, it is natural to raise the question: "Can the context of correlative local interest points be integrated to detect more meaningful and discriminative features?"

In this chapter, we explore the "context" issue of local feature detectors, which refers to both spatial and inter-image concurrence statistics of local features. We first review related works on how the local feature context can benefit visual representation and recognition. In general, works in this field can be subdivided into three groups:

- The methods to combine spatial contexts to build local descriptors [19, 85–89]. For example, the shape context idea [19] adopted spatially nearby shape primitives to co-describe local shape features by radial and directive bin division. Lazebnik et al. [87] presented a semi-local affine part description, which used geometric construction and supervised grouping of local affine parts to model 3D objects. Bileschi et al. [89] proposed a contextual description with continuity, symmetry, closure, and repetition to low-level descriptors, with the C1 feature as its basic detector part.
- The methods to combine spatial contexts to refine the recognition classifiers. The most representative work comes from that of Torralba et al. [90–92] in context-aware recognition, aiming to integrate spatial co-occurrence statistics into recognition classifier outputs to co-determine object labels. In addition to these two groups, there are also recent works in context-aware similarity matching [35, 93], which adopts similarities from spatial neighbors to filter out contextually dissimilar patches. It

has been shown that by combining the contextual statistics of the local descriptors, the overall discriminability can be largely improved.

- The methods related to biological-inspired models to filter out non-informative regions with limited saliency [94]. Serre et al. [95] presented a biological-inspired model to mirror the mechanisms of V1 and V2 cortices, in which a "S1-C1-S2-C2" framework is proposed to extract features.

The proposed feature detector consists of two steps: First, at a given scale, the correlation among spatially nearby local interest points are modeled, with a Gaussian kernel to build a contextual response. We simulate the Gaussian smoothing and call the output of this step contextual Gaussian estimator. Then, following the difference of Gaussians setting, we derive the difference between nearby scales, which are aggregated into a difference of contextual Gaussians (DoCG) field. We show that the DoCG field can highlight contextually salient regions, as well as discriminate foreground regions from background clutter to reveal visual attention [94, 96]. The proposed "semi-local" detector is built over the peaks in the DoCG field, which is achieved by locating contextual peaks using mean shift search [37]. Each located peak is described with a context-aware semi-local descriptor, which meanwhile ensures the invariance to scales, rotations, and affine transformations.

We further extend our semi-local interest-point detector from the unsupervised case to the supervised case. In the literature, this is related to visual pattern mining [71, 72, 97] or learning-based descriptors [22, 23]. Notably, our work serves as the first one targeted at "learning-based interest-point detection" to the best of our knowledge. This is achieved by integrating category learning into our mean shift search kernels and weights to discover category-aware discriminative features.

This chapter serves as the basis for the entire book about learning-based visual local representation and indexing: First, at the initial local interest-point detection stage, it is beneficial to embed spatial nearest neighbor cues as context to design a better detector, which can serve as a good initial step for the subsequent unsupervised or supervised codebook learning. Second, the learned "semi-local" interest-point detector can be further used in many other application scenarios, to be combined with other related techniques to directly improve retrieval, as will be detailed later in this chapter. For more details and innovations of this chapter, please refer to our publication in ACM Transactions on Intelligent Systems and Technology (2012).

2.2 DIFFERENCE OF CONTEXTUAL GAUSSIANS

We first introduce how to build the local detector context based on their spatial co-occurrence statistics at multiple scales. General speaking, the "base" detector can be any of the current approaches [81]. As an example, here we use difference of Gaussians [9] as the base detector.

2.2.1 Local Interest-Point Detection

For a target image, we first define the scale space L at scale δ by applying a Gaussian convolution kernel to the intensity component in its HSI color space. As shown in Equation (2.1), $I(x,y)$ stands for the Intensity of pixel (x,y) and $G(x,y,\delta)$ is a Gaussian kernel applied to (x,y) with scale parameter δ:

$$L(x,y,\delta) = G(x,y,\delta) * I(x,y). \tag{2.1}$$

Then, we calculate the difference of Gaussians at the kth scale by subtracting the Gaussian convolutions between the kth scale $k\delta$ and the original scale δ (which produce scale spaces $L(x,y,k\delta)$ and $L(x,y,\delta)$, respectively):

$$\begin{aligned} D(x,y,\delta) &= (G(x,y,k\delta) - G(x,y,\delta)) * I(x,y) \\ &= L(x,y,k\delta) - L(x,y,\delta). \end{aligned} \tag{2.2}$$

Finally, we identify the local feature candidates as the local maxima within their space and scale neighbors. For a given (x,y) location, there are $3 \times 9 - 1$ neighbors in total. For each candidate, we construct a Hessian matrix to investigate the ratio between its trace square and determinant. This ratio removes candidates coming from edge points with only signal changes in one dimension. We use the SIFT [9] descriptor to describe each remaining candidate as a 128-dimension local feature vector S. Similarly, other current descriptors [10] can be also adopted.

2.2.2 Accumulating Contextual Gaussian Difference

Then, the distribution of local feature context is quantitatively measured using a proposed difference of contextual Gaussians DoCG field: Our main idea is to estimate the contextual intensity of local features (named contextual Gaussian) based on their spatial distributions with other Gaussian kernel smoothing at different scales. The differences between contextual Gaussian at different scales are then aggregated to produce the DoCG field to quantize the local feature context.

Based upon the above principle, we give detailed formulation as follows: For a given local feature at location (x, y), its contextual Gaussian response is estimated using its neighborhood local feature distributions with Gaussian smoothing at "contextual" scale $\delta_{context}$:

$$S_{CL}(x, y, \delta_{context})$$
$$= \frac{1}{n} \sum_{i=1}^{n} \frac{1}{2\pi \delta_{context}^2} e^{-\frac{(x-x_i)^2+(y-y_i)^2}{2\delta_{context}^2}} S_i, \tag{2.3}$$

where $S_{CL}(x, y, \delta_{context})$ is the estimated contextual Gaussian density at location (x, y) with contextual scale $\delta_{context}$; $i = 1$ to n represents the n local features falling within $\delta_{context}$ of (x, y); and S_i is the feature vector of the ith neighborhood local feature descriptor.

We then calculate the difference of contextual Gaussians (S_{DoCG}) at the kth scale ($k\delta_{context}$) by subtracting $S_{CL}(x, y, k\delta_{context})$ and $S_{CL}(x, y, \delta_{context})$ between the $k\delta_{context}$ and the $\delta_{context}$ contextual scales:

$$S_{DoCG}(x, y, k\delta_{context})$$
$$= \frac{1}{n'} \sum_{j=1}^{n'} \frac{1}{2\pi (k\delta_{context})^2} e^{-\frac{((x-x_j)^2+(y-y_j)^2)}{2(k\delta_{context})^2}} S_j$$
$$- \frac{1}{n} \sum_{i=1}^{n} \frac{1}{2\pi \delta_{context}^2} e^{-\frac{((x-x_i)^2+(y-y_i)^2)}{2\delta_{context}^2}} S_i \tag{2.4}$$
$$= S_{CL}(x, y, k\delta_{context}) - S_{CL}(x, y, \delta_{context}).$$

Note that the above operation differs from the traditional DoG operation [8] which seeks the neighborhood local peaks within the consecutive scales. In contrast, we accumulate the difference of contextual Gaussians between different scales[1] additively to produce a final DoCG field, denoted as $S_{DoCG}(x, y)$:

$$S_{DoCG}(x, y) = \sum_{k=1}^{K} S_{DoCG}(x, y, k\delta_{context}). \tag{2.5}$$

Similar to DoG, this accumulated response $S_{DoCG}(x, y)$ among all scales can indicate the robustness of location (x, y) to the variances caused by scale variances.

---

[1] There are in total $(K - 1)$ accumulations for K scales.

2.3 MEAN SHIFT-BASED LOCALIZATION

2.3.1 Localization Algorithm

We further detect the semi-local salient regions over the local detector context. This detection is achieved by mean shift search [37] over the DoCG field to discover semi-local contextual peaks. The mean shift vector for each location (x, y) is calculated as:

$$M(S_{\textbf{DoCG}}(x, y))$$

$$= \frac{\sum_{i=1}^{n} G_H(S_{\textbf{DoCG}}^i - S_{\textbf{DoCG}}) w(S_{\textbf{DoCG}}^i)(S_{\textbf{DoCG}}^i - S_{\textbf{DoCG}})}{\sum_{i=1}^{n} G_H(S_{\textbf{DoCG}}^i - S_{\textbf{DoCG}}) w(S_{\textbf{DoCG}}^i)}. \tag{2.6}$$

In Equation (2.6), $w(S_{\textbf{DoCG}}^i) \geqslant 0$ is the weight given to the *ith* local feature, $i = 1$ to n denotes the n local features that fall within $G_H()$ of (x, y), and $G_H()$ is a Gaussian kernel that differentiates contributions of different local features based on their distances from (x, y). We denote $G_H(S_{\textbf{DoCG}} - S_{\textbf{DoCG}})$ as:

$$G_H(S_{\textbf{DoCG}}^i - S_{\textbf{DoCG}})$$

$$= |H|^{-1/2} G(|H|^{-1/2}(S_{\textbf{DoCG}}^i - S_{\textbf{DoCG}})). \tag{2.7}$$

H is a positive definite $d \times d$ bandwidth matrix. We simplify H as a diagonal matrix $(diag[h_1^2, \ldots, h_d^2])$.

Equation (2.6) can be further converted into:

$$M_h(S_{\textbf{DoCG}}(x, y))$$

$$= \frac{\sum_{i=1}^{n} G_H(S_{\textbf{DoCG}}^i - S_{\textbf{DoCG}}) w(S_{\textbf{DoCG}}^i) S_{\textbf{DoCG}}^i}{\sum_{i=1}^{n} G_H(S_{\textbf{DoCG}}^i - S_{\textbf{DoCG}}) w(S_{\textbf{DoCG}}^i)} - S_{\textbf{DoCG}} \tag{2.8}$$

$$= m_h(S_{\textbf{DoCG}}(x, y)) - S_{\textbf{DoCG}}.$$

We denote the first term in the second line of Equation (2.8) as $m_h(S_{\textbf{DoCG}}(x, y))$, which represents the gradient of the DoCG field at the point (x, y) are conducted. Subsequently, the mean shift search for contextual peaks over the DoCG field are conducted as:

- **Step 1**: Compute $m_h(S_{\textbf{DoCG}}(x, y))$ to offer certain robustness to ensure feature locating precision.

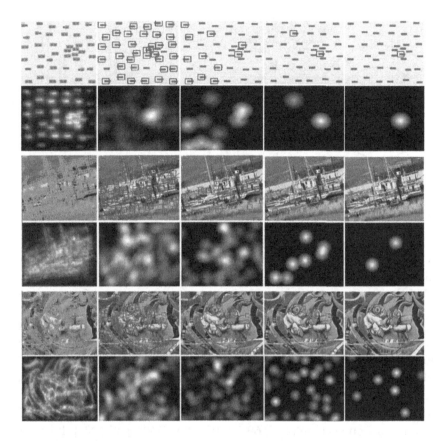

Figure 2.1 Influences of different contextual and Mean Shift scales.

- **Step 2**: Assign the nearest SIFT point as a new (x, y) position to $m_h(S_{DoCG}(x, y))$ for the next-round iteration.
- **Step 3**: If $||m_h(S_{DoCG}(x, y)) - S_{DoCG}|| \leq \varepsilon$, stop its mean shift operation; otherwise, repeat Step 1.

The final convergence is achieved at local maximal or minimal locations in the DoCG field, which are defined as the detected locations of our CASL detector.

Figure 2.1 further shows the effect of tuning both contextual and mean shift scales (in each contextual scale, we settle the mean shift scale by adding 30 additional pixels) to achieve local-to-global context detections. Please note that tuning larger contextual and mean shift scales (e.g., to include all SIFT features into contextual representation) would result in focusing

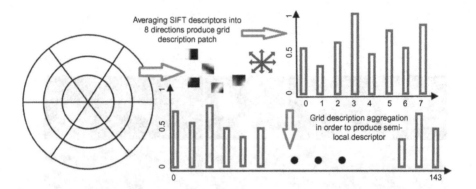

Figure 2.2 Proposed descriptor for CASL detectors.

attention on viewing images. On the contrary, small contextual and mean shift scales degenerate CASL into a traditional local feature detector (e.g., SIFT [9]).

To further describe the detected feature, we follow the design of shape context: First, we provide a polar-grid division for context-aware description. A visualized example of our descriptor is shown in Figure 2.2. For each semi-local interest point, we include the local features in its $\delta_{Context}$ neighbor into its description. We subdivide these $\delta_{Context}$ neighbors into log-polar grids with 3 bins in radial directions (radius: 6, 11, and 15 pixels) and 6 in angular directions (angle: 0°, 60°, 120°, 180°, 240°, and 300°). It results in a 17-bin division. The central bin is not divided in angular directions to offer a certain robustness against feature locating precisions, which differs from GLOH [10]. In each grid, the gradient orientations of SIFT points are averaged and quantized in 8 bins. It produces a $(3 \times 6 \times 8)$ 144-bin histogram for each CASE descriptor.

2.3.2 Comparison to Saliency

Different from the traditional local salient region detectors [8, 29, 80, 81], our semi-local detector can discover salient regions based on the DoCG field construction, which is a key advantage compared to the current works. Indeed, we have discovered that the high response locations for DoCG shares good similarity to visual saliency detection results. We explain this phenomenon from the construction process of the DoCG field: For a given location, our semi-local contextual measurement is derived by accumulating differences of co-occurrence strengths among K contextual scales. Similarly, the principle of a spatial saliency map [94] adopts a center-surround difference operation to discover highly contrasted points at different scales with Gaussian smoothing, which are then fused to evaluate point saliency. From another viewpoint, the DoCG field also shares certain similarity with the spectral saliency map [96] built by the Fourier transform, which retains the global spectrum phase to evaluate pixel saliency. In comparison, based on spatial convolution and difference accumulation, our DoCG field also preserves global character in general, for which the high-frequency fluctuations are discarded by spatial Gaussian convolutions over local feature densities, and the influences of frequency variances are further weakened by the different operations of contextual strengths. Notably, the "center-surround" operation is the basic and fundamental form of "context", which is similar to many "center-surround" saliency detection operations [94].

2.4 DETECTOR LEARNING

We further extend our detector design from the unsupervised case to the supervised case. In such a case, different from the traditional local feature detectors that perform in an unsupervised manner, our CASL detector also enables learning-based detection when there are multiple images available from an identical category.

In this setting, multiple images from the same category are available, which are treated as a whole in detection. For each image within this given category, we integrate semi-local statistics from other images to "teach" the CASL detector to locate category-aware semi-local peaks, which removes the features that are useless in discriminating this category from the others. This is achieved by refining the mean shift kernels and weights in the second phase of our CASL detector.

First, we adopt k-means clustering to group local features extracted from (1) the category images, or (2) the entire image dataset containing categories (if other images are also available). Subsequently, we build a bag-of-visual-words [16] model from the clustering results to produce a visual word signature for each local feature. For each visual word, its term frequency (TF) [28] weighting is calculated to describe its importance (within this category) in constructing S_{DoCG}. This importance modifies the weight $w(S^i_{\text{DoCG}})$ and kernel $G_H(S^i_{\text{DoCG}} - S_{\text{DoCG}})$ in the mean shift search (Equation (2.6)). Figure 2.3 shows some detection examples.

Figure 2.3 Results of learning-based CASL detection.

To determine the mean shift search weight in Equation (2.6), the following modification is made:

$$w(S_{\mathbf{DoCG}}^i) = \frac{n_j}{N_{\text{Total}}^C},$$ (2.9)

in which the ith local feature belongs to the *jth* visual word; n_j represents the number of local features that both belong to the *j*th visual word and are within the current image category; and N_{Total}^C represents the total number of local features that are extracted from images of this category.

Given the labels of images belonging to the other categories, we further incorporate inter-category statistics, together with the former intra-category statistics, to build our learning-based CASL detector. This is achieved by introducing an inverted document weighting scheme [28] to improve the $w(S_{\mathbf{DoCG}}^i)$ in Equation (2.6):

$$w(S_{\mathbf{DoCG}}^i) = \frac{n_j}{N_{\text{Total}}^C} \times log(\frac{N_{\text{Total}}}{N_{\text{Total}}^C}),$$ (2.10)

in which N_{Total} represents the number of SIFT features extracted from the entire image database, which contains multiple image categories (the current category C is one of these categories).

The learning is achieved by refining the mean shift search kernel in Equation (2.6). The following modifications are made onto the positive definite bandwidth matrix H, which is simplified as a diagonal matrix $diag[h_1^2, \ldots, h_d^2]$ (d is the dimension of the local feature descriptors, such as 128 for SIFT) into:

$$diag[(wF_1 \times h_1)^2, (wF_2 \times h_2)^2, \ldots, (wF_d \times h_d)^2]. \qquad (2.11)$$

The weight wF for each dimension h_i is determined by Fisher discriminant analysis [98] as:

$$wF_i = \frac{D_{\text{Between}}}{D_{\text{Within}}} = \frac{(m_i - m'_i)(m_i - m'_i)}{\frac{1}{C} \sum_{s \in C} (s_i - m_1)(s_i - m_1)^t}, \qquad (2.12)$$

where wF_i denotes the weight for the ith dimension d_i and D_{Between} and D_{Within} represent the between-category distance and within-category distance, respectively. We estimate the mean value of the ith dimension from both images within this category (m_i) and images randomly sampled outside this category (m'_i) with the same volume (denoted as N_c in Equation (2.12)). These values are then subdivided to obtain D_{Between} (calculated by ($m_i - m'_i)(m_i - m'_i)$). Similarly, the variance of this dimension is obtained as its averaged intra-category distance ($\frac{1}{N_c} \sum_{s \in C} (s_i - m_1)(s_i - m_1)^t$).

We briefly review the connection between the proposed supervised CASL and other feature learning schemes as follows:

- Former works in learning-based local feature representation can be categorized into two groups. The first group aims to learn local feature descriptors [22, 23], which uses a ground truth set of matching correspondences (pairs of matched features) to learn descriptor parameters. Due to the requirement of "exact" matching correspondences, works in [22, 23] can be viewed as a strongly supervised learning scenario. On the contrary, our learning-based CASL only requires image category information rather than exact matching correspondences and hence can be viewed as a weakly supervised learning scenario.
- The second group derives from the frequent visual pattern mining [71, 72, 97], which adopts spatial association rules to mine frequent patterns (defined as certain spatial combinations of visual words in [71, 72, 97]). Our main advantages lie in the efficiency: Works in [71, 72, 97] all require the time-consuming frequent item set mining,

Figure 2.4 Examples from the UKBench retrieval benchmark database.

such as the A-prior co-location pattern mining [99], to find meaningful patterns.

- Last and most important, our approach puts forward the learning mechanism into the feature detection step (mean shift over DoCG), which enables us to discover category-aware locations during feature detection. This differs from all related works in learning-based description [22, 23] or feature selection [71, 72, 97].

2.5 EXPERIMENTS

This section presents the quantitative experimental evaluations of our CASL detector with comparisons to current approaches. First, to prove that our CASL detector can still maintain good detection repeatability without regard to photometric variations, we give a series of standardized evaluations in the INRIA detector evaluation sequences [100]. Second, to demonstrate our effectiveness in discovering discriminative and meaningful interest points, we evaluate our CASL detector in two challenging computer vision tasks: (1) near-duplicated image retrieval in UKBench [16] as shown in Figure 2.4 and (2) object categorization in Caltech101, as shown in Figure 2.5.

2.5.1 Database and Evaluation Criteria
Despite detecting meaningful and discriminative salient regions, we should still ensure that our CASL detector can well retain the detector repeatability requirement [100], which is crucial for many computer

Figure 2.5 Examples from the Caltech101 object categorization database.

vision applications, such as image matching and 3D scene modeling. We evaluated our detector repeatability in the INRIA detector evaluation sequences [100]. Using this database, we directly got the results reported in [100] as our baselines. In [100], the repeatability rate of detected regions among a test image t and the *ith* image in the test sequence are calculated as:

$$Repeatability(t, i) = \frac{|R_I(\epsilon)|}{min(n_t, n_i)}, \qquad (2.13)$$

in which the $|R_I(\epsilon)|$ denotes the number of $\epsilon_{repeatable}$ [100] salient regions between t and i and the n_t and n_i represents the number of salient regions detected in the common part of images t and i, respectively. Refer to [100] for detailed experimental setups.

We adopted the UKBench benchmark database [16] to evaluate the effectiveness of our CASL detector in the near-duplicated image retrieval task. The UKBench database contains 10,000 images with 2,500 objects.

There are four images per object to offer sufficient variances in viewpoints, rotations, lighting conditions, scales, occlusions, and affine transforms.

We built our retrieval model over the entire UKBench database. Then we selected the first image per object to form a query set to test our performance. This experimental setup is identical to [16], which directly offers us the baseline performance of MSER + SIFT reported in [16]. Identical to [16], we ensured that the top returning photo would be the query itself, hence the performance depends on whether the system can return the remaining three photos of this object as early as possible. This criterion was measured as the "Correct Returning" in [16].

We selected a 10-category subset of Caltech101 database to evaluate our CASL detector in the object categorization task, including *face, car side, snoopy, elephant, wheelchair, cellphone, motorbike, butterfly, pyramid*, and *buddha*. Each image category contains approximately 60 to 90 images. We randomly selected 10 images from each category to form a test set, and used the rest of the images to train the classifiers.

We evaluated our categorization performance by measuring the percentage of corrected categorizations in each category (averaged hit/miss of its 10 test examples) to draw a categorization confused matrix.

There are five groups of baselines in our experimental comparisons.

1. *Local Detectors*: First, we offer four baselines of local detectors, including DoG [8], MSER [29], Harris-Affine [80], and Hessian-Affine [81].
2. *Local Descriptors*: Second, we offer two baselines of local descriptors, i.e., SIFT [9] and GLOH [10] (for comparison to the CASE descriptor).
3. *Saliency Map Pre-Filtering*: In both comparisons, we also compare with the saliency map pre-filtering [94] to select salient local features.
4. *Integration of Category Learning*: Third, we compare our learning-based CASL detector + SVM with two baselines of both CASL (without learning) + SVM and Bag-of-Visual-Words (SIFT) + SVM in the object categorization task.
5. *Context-Aware Features*: Finally, we compare our framework with two context-aware feature representations: (1) the "S1-C1-S2-C2" global contextual features [95] and (2) the Shape Context features [19] in both Caltech6 and Caltech101 recognition benchmark databases.

2.5.2 Detector Repeatability

Figure 2.6 shows the quantitative evaluations of the detector repeatability comparisons in the sequences of different *scales, viewpoints, blurs, compressions,* and *illuminations.* We can see that our CASL detector produces more repeatable detection results in the repeatability comparisons of *compressions, illuminations,* and *blurs.* And we obtain comparable performances in the repeatability comparisons of *viewpoints* and *scales.* Although our CASL detector produces generally fewer salient regions compared with the alterative approaches, we still achieve comparable performance by including semi-local spatial layouts in detection. Such spatial layout prevents unstable detections that are frequently found in traditional local feature detectors.

Figure 2.6 shows the quantitative evaluations of the detector repeatability comparisons in the sequences of different scales, viewpoints, blurs, compressions, and illuminations. We can see that, in many cases, our CASL detector produces more repeatable detection results in the repeatability comparisons of illuminations (fifth subfigure) and viewpoints (sixth subfigure); in all cases better in the repeatability comparisons of compressions (fourth subfigure); and in some cases better in the repeatability comparisons of blurs (third subfigure). However, we should note that we almost rank persistently worse than the Hessian-affine in viewpoints (first subfigure) and scales (second subfigure) (Hessian-affine is shown as one of the most effective detectors in the literature). One reason for this performance is that our CASL detector generally produces fewer salient regions, compared with the alternative approaches. In summary, our CASL detector achieves comparable performance to current detectors with generally fewer features per image. It could be due to including semi-local spatial layouts into detection. Such spatial layout prevents unstable detections that are frequently found in the traditional local features detectors. However, as shown in Figure 2.6, in some cases such as viewpoints or scales changes, Hessian-affine and MSER would be a better choice due to their simplicity.

We further compare the computational time cost of our CASL detector with respect to different contextual scales and mean shift scales in Table 2.1. One interesting observation here is that by increasing both contextual and mean shift scale, the overall computational cost will subsequently increase.

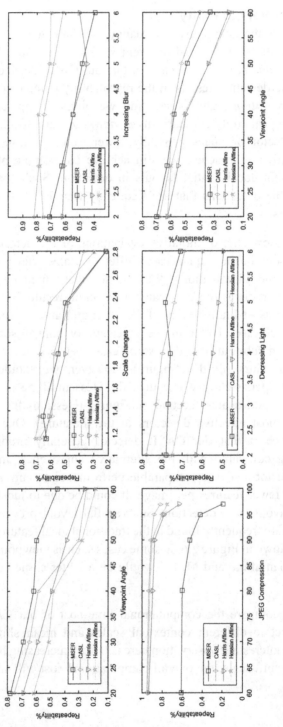

Figure 2.6 Repeatability comparison in detector repeatability sequence.

Table 2.1 Influence of different contextual scales S_c and Mean Shift scales S_m

Time Cost	$S_c = 10$	$S_c = 15$	$S_c = 20$	$S_c = 25$	$S_c = 30$
$S_m = 30$	1.25s	1.36s	1.78s	2.23s	2.55s
$S_m = 40$	1.71s	1.98s	2.06s	2.38s	2.68s
$S_m = 50$	2.16s	2.12s	2.65s	2.97s	3.54s
$S_m = 60$	2.29s	2.49s	3.12s	3.41s	3.68s

2.5.3 CASL for Image Search and Classification

Note that in all methods, the "correct returning" is larger than 1, since the query would definitely find itself in the database. This experimental setup is identical to [16], which directly offers us the baseline performance of MSER + SIFT reported in [16]. We provide three implementation approaches: CASL (local detector part: DoG + SIFT) + SIFT, CASL (local detector part: MSER + SIFT) + SIFT, CASL (local detector part: DoG + SIFT) + CASE, CASL (local detector part: MSER + SIFT) + CASE; CASL (local detector part: DoG + MOP) + CASE, CASL (local detector part: MSER + MOP) + CASE. The experimental results show that in the local feature building block of CASL, the DoG + SIFT is a better choice for the task of near-duplicated image retrieval.

We built a 10-branch, 4-layer dictionary tree (VT) [16] for the UKbench database, which produced approximately 10,000 visual words. Nearly 450,000 CASL features and nearly 1,370,000 MSER + SIFT features were extracted from the entire database to build two vocabulary tree models [16], respectively (with inverted document indexing), each of which gave a bag-of-visual-words (BoW) vector [16] for each image. In the vocabulary tree model, if features within a node were less than a given threshold (100 for CASL features, 250 for SIFT features), we stopped the k-means division of this node, whether it had reached the deepest level or not. For a a-branch VT with m words, the search time for one feature point is $a \log_a(m)$, which is proportional to the logarithm of branch number, and is independent of the database volume.

Figure 2.7 shows the performance of CASL + CASE in comparison with state-of-the-art local feature detectors (DoG, MSER), descriptors (SIFT), and the improvement based on saliency map pre-filtering:

1. DoG [8] + SIFT [9], a widely adopted approach to building a bag-of-visual-words model.

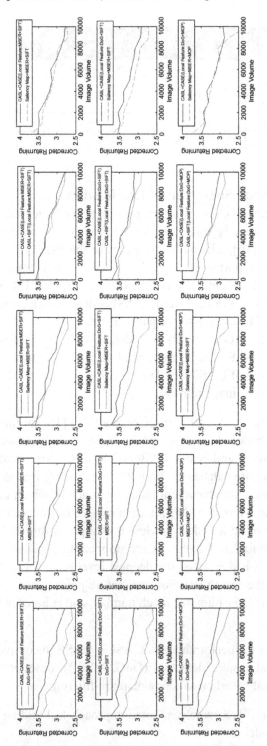

Figure 2.7 CASL performance comparison in near-duplicated image retrieval.

2. MSER [29] + SIFT [9], which is the implementation of a vocabulary tree model [16] in near-duplicated search.

3. Saliency map [94] + MSER [29] + SIFT [9], in which we maintain only salient local features (measured by pixel-level saliency for a detected local feature location) to build the subsequent dictionary.

4. CASL + SIFT [9], which quantize the performance of our CASE descriptor.

5. DoG + MOP [21] as an alternative approach for our implemental baseline of DoG + SIFT [9]. However, as shown in Figure 2.7, this is a suboptimal choice for our subsequent CASL feature construction.

6. MSER [29] + MOP [21] as another alternative approach for our implemental baseline of DoG + SIFT [9]. Similarly, as shown in Figure 2.7, this is also a suboptimal choice for our subsequent CASL feature construction.

All these methods are based on the bag-of-visual-words quantization in which we adopt an inverted document search to find the near-duplicated images of the query example (in our query set) on the UKBench database.

From Figure 2.7, it is obvious that our CASL feature outperforms baseline methods that are based solely on local features with saliency map pre-filtering. Meanwhile, comparing with MSER [29], DoG [8] performs much better in building our local feature context.

Higher precisions also indicate two merits of our CASL detector: (1) More repeatability over rotation, scale, and affine transformations, which are common in the UKBench database; and (2) more discrimination within different object appearances. The photos in UKBench usually contain different objects such as CD covers with identical or near duplicated backgrounds. Hence, the capability to discriminate a foreground object from background clutter is essential for high performance.

For the task of object recognition, we built a 2-layer, 30-branch vocabulary tree [16] for image indexing, which contains approximately 900 visual words for this categorization task. For each category, the bag-of-visual-words vectors (approximately 900 dimensions for each image) are extracted for training. We offline built a SVM for every two categories. In the online recognition, we adopted a one-vs-one strategy to vote for the category membership for a test image: If one category won a SVM between this category and another category, we increased the voting score for the winning category by one. The category with the highest scores was assigned

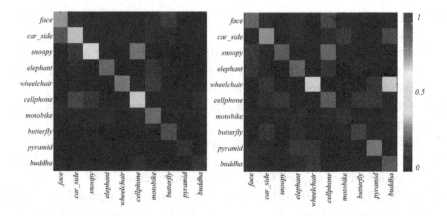

Figure 2.8 Categorization confusion matrix in 10 categories from Caltech101 (I).

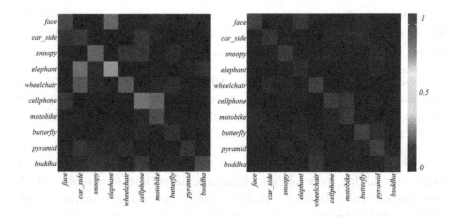

Figure 2.9 Categorization confusion matrix in 10 categories from Caltech101 (II).

to the test image as its final label. Since we aimed to compare CASL with other detectors, we simply adopted a one-vs-one SVM in the classifier phase, which can be easily replaced by other sophisticated methods, e.g., SVM-KNN. We used the same parameter tuning approach described for near-duplicated image retrieval to tune the best contextual and mean shift scales.

Figures 2.8–2.9 present the confused matrix of different combination schemes, including (1) Saliency map + MSER + SIFT + SVM, (2) CASL (local features: MSER + SIFT) + CASE + SVM, (3) CASL (local features: DoG + SIFT) + CASE + SVM, and (4) learning-based CASL (local features:

Table 2.2 Quantitative comparisons to contextual global features in Caltech5 subset

SIFT+SVM		C2 Feature [95]+SVM		CASL+SVM	
Category	Pre	Category	Pre	Category	Pre
Airplanes	85	Airplanes	95	Airplanes	**96**
Leaves	86	Leaves	**96**	Leaves	**96**
Motorcycles	**99**	Motorcycles	97	Motorcycles	98
Face	83	Face	**98**	Face	**98**
Cars	96	Cars	**99**	Cars	96

DoG + SIFT) + CASE + SVM. Generally speaking, CASL features perform much better than the approach that adopted saliency map pre-filtering to integrate semi-local cues. Meanwhile, the integration of learning part into CASL detector can largely boost the categorization performance in our current settlement.

We give quantitative comparisons to the context-aware global features [95]. Identical to the settlement of [95], the Caltech5 is adopted in comparison. The performances of SIFT and C2 are directly from [95], the former of which adopted approximately 1,000-dimension features for categorization. To offer comparable evaluations, we built a CASL-based BoW vector containing about 900 visual words, and adopted linear SVM for classifier training. Note that we also used learning-based CASL in feature extraction.

Based on the comparison in the Caltech5 database (Table 2.2), our CASL detector achieved almost identical performance to the best performance reported in [95]. Since C2 +SVM already achieves very high (nearly 100 percent) performance, it is hard to obtain much better performance with a large margin. On the contrary, in addition to (slightly) better performance for C2 features, our CASL detector also shows much better results than SIFT + SVM with a large margin. Nevertheless, the C2 feature is better at higher computational cost. However, there are two major differences between our approach and the S1-C1-S2-C2 features [95]:

First, the S1-C1-S2-C2-like feature extraction and classification framework [95] produces one feature vector per image with fixed feature dimension. This is different from our CASL detector that outputs patch-based features to produce bag-of-(semi-local)-word representations.

Table 2.3 Quantitative comparisons to Shape Context in Caltech5 subset (classification phase: SVM)

SIFT		CASL+Shape Context		CASL+CASE	
Category	Pre	Category	Pre	Category	Pre
Airplanes	85	Airplanes	92	Airplanes	**96**
Leaves	86	Leaves	86	Leaves	**96**
Motorcycles	**99**	Motorcycles	88	Motorcycles	98
Face	83	Face	84	Face	**98**
Cars	96	Cars	89	Cars	96

Table 2.4 Time cost comparisons of different contextual scales (S_c) and mean shift scales (S_m)

Time Cost	$S_c = 10$	$S_c = 15$	$S_c = 20$	$S_c = 25$	$S_c = 30$
$S_m = 30$	1.25s	1.36s	1.78s	2.23s	2.55s
$S_m = 40$	1.71s	1.98s	2.06s	2.38s	2.68s
$S_m = 50$	2.16s	2.12s	2.65s	2.97s	3.54s
$S_m = 60$	2.29s	2.49s	3.12s	3.41s	3.68s

Second, the S2-C2 part in [95] needs training for prototype learning, which is indispensable in feature construction. In contrast, our CASL feature can also perform in an unsupervised manner (the learning is an optional choice), which can be easily reapplied into other unsupervised scenarios, and can be further combined with more complicated classifiers in the subsequent categorization step.

Regarding the polar-bin division strategy, there exists similarity between our CASE descriptor and the shape context feature [19]. Hence, it is a natural to replace our CASE descriptor with the shape context descriptor. Table 2.3 presents the experimental comparisons of our CASL + CASE feature with the CASL + shape context feature [19]. We should note that the shape context is a feature descriptor, which is not competitive but comprehensive to our CASL detector. However, we have found that the direct replacement of the shape context feature to our CASE descriptor cannot achieve satisfactory results for our CASL detections. Its similarity matching mechanisms are originally designed for shape primitives (Table 2.4).

Based on the above three groups of experiments with comparisons to current technology, we have the following statements and guidelines about our application scenarios:

(1) What vision tasks are more suitable for CASL than traditional local feature detectors?

- The vision tasks emphasize discovering meaningful and discriminative features, rather than repeatable detection. For instance, generalized or specialized object recognition, image annotation, semantic understanding, and video concept detection.
- CASL is also suitable for the case where more attentional focus is needed, such as to describe images based solely on the most salient objects, or to discriminate foreground objects from backgrounds from a set of training images. In the latter case, we should also know their category labels beforehand to carry out our learning-based CASL.

(2) What scenarios are not as suitable for CASL instead of local feature detectors?

- When the vision tasks emphasize the repeatable detection more, rather than semantic or attentional discriminability, e.g., image matching and wide baseline matching.
- When the target image contains large amount of local features, and there are no demands to differentiate the foreground object from background clutter. For instance, scene matching and near-duplicated scene identification.

2.6 SUMMARY

This chapter gave a systematic exploration of context information in designing interest point detector. Going beyond current approaches, we integrated contextual cues to enhance the interest point detector from a traditional local scale to a "semi-local" scale, which enabled us to discover more meaningful and discriminative salient regions without losing detector repeatability. Our other contribution here was to introduce a learning-based detector mechanism. It introduces the category learning (traditionally in subsequent classifier phases) into the feature detection phase, which locates category-aware interest points to improve performance of the subsequent recognition classifiers.

All of these contributions are integrated within a novel context-aware semi-local (CASL) feature detector framework, which is a two-step procedure: The first step builds the local feature context-based on a proposed difference of contextual Gaussians DoCG field, which offers the capability to highlight attentional salient regions, sharing good similarity with the saliency map detection results. The second step adopts a mean shift search to locate semi-local DoCG peaks as context-aware salient regions. This step naturally enables learning-based detection by integrating category learning into the mean shift weights and kernels. We conducted quantitative comparisons on image search, object categorization, and detector repeatability evaluations. We compared our performance with current approaches, based on which we further discussed the suitable and unsuitable scenarios for deploying our CASL detector.

Two interesting questions remain: First, we would further integrate category learning into the DoCG construction phase, in which we can adopt category-aware distributions to supervise the contextual representation of local features. Second, we are interested in extending our CASL feature to detect context-aware 3D salient regions within videos, in which we would investigate whether the sequential characteristics of successive frames can be used to construct the spatiotemporal contextual statistics in our first phase. The related work of this chapter is published in *ACM Transactions on Intelligent Systems and Technology.*

CHAPTER 3

Unsupervised Dictionary Optimization

3.1 INTRODUCTION

This chapter introduces density-based metric learning (DML) to refine the similarity metric in hierarchical clustering, which makes middle level words to be effective in retrieval. Based on an optimized VT model, we propose a novel idea to leverage the tree hierarchy in a vertical boosting chain manner [84] to improve retrieval effectiveness. Furthermore, we also demonstrate that exploiting the VT hierarchy can improve its generativity across different databases. We propose a "VT shift" algorithm to *transfer* a vocabulary tree model into new databases, which efficiently maintains considerable performance without reclustering. Our proposed VT shift algorithm also enables incremental indexing of the vocabulary tree for a changing database. In this case our algorithm can efficiently register new images into the database without regenerating an entire model from the overall database. For more detailed innovations of this chapter, please refer to our publication in IEEE International Conference on Computer Vision and Pattern Recognition 2009.

How Hierarchical Structure Affects VT-based Retrieval: Papers [31, 36] have shown that the k-means process would drift clusters to denser regions due to its "mean-shift"-like updating rule, which results in asymmetry division of feature space. We have found out that the hierarchical structure of VT would iteratively magnify such asymmetry division. More hierarchy levels result in more asymmetric similarity metrics in clustering. Therefore, the distribution of "visual words" would bias to denser regions in feature space (similar to random sampling), or even over-fit to feature density. However, to guarantee good "visual words" in hierarchical clustering, denser regions should correspond to more generic image patches, while sparser regions should be more discriminative. Recall that in TF-IDF the term weighting a visual word gains less weight when it appears in more images and vice versa. Hence, the hierarchical construction of VT would severely bias feature quantization: The discriminative patches (sparser regions that rarely appear in many images) would be coarsely quantized (i.e., give lower IDF and contribute less in ranking), while the general patches

Table 3.1 Hierarchical quantization errors measured using the overlapping rates (%)

NN / GNP	1	3	5	10	15	20
50	41.46%	73.34%	85.00%	94.53%	97.11%	98.18%
200	57.46%	66.21%	79.00%	92.02%	95.00%	97.48%
1,000	11.54%	38.27%	51.57%	67.48%	85.16%	94.91%
2,000	6.38%	25.68%	40.59%	58.54%	79.21%	92.42%

(denser regions that frequently appear in many images) would be finely quantized (i.e., gain inappropriately higher IDF in ranking). This is exactly the reason for inefficient IDF in [30] and [32]. In our consideration, the IDF inefficiency lies in the biased similarity metric, which is magnified by hierarchy clustering.

Another issue is that the nearest neighbor search within leaf nodes is inaccurate due to its local nature in the hierarchical tree structure, which would also degenerate matching accuracy. For validation, we compare the matching ratio of nearest neighbor search results both inside leaves and among overall feature space. For the vocabulary tree, the nearest neighbor search in leaf nodes is more inaccurate as the increase of nearest neighbor number in search scope. For validation, we compare the matching ratio of nearest neighbor (NN) search results both inside leaves and among overall feature space.

Table 3.1 presents the investigation of quantization errors in a 3-branch, 5-level vocabulary tree. We select 3K images from our urban street scene database to form the VT, with 0.5M features (average of 2K features in each visual word). We compare the matching ratio between global-scale NN and leaf-scale NN, in which global-scale is in the overall feature space while the leaf-scale is inside the leaf nodes.

Greedy N-best Path

We extend the leaf-scale to include more local neighbors using greedy N-best path (GNP) [27]. The quantization error is evaluated by the matching ratio (%) to see to what extent the VT quantization would cause feature point mismatching (Figure 3.1). In Table 3.1, NN means the nearest neighbor search scope and GNP 1–5 means the numbers of branches we parallel in the GNP search extension. From Table 3.1 the match ratios between the inside-leaf and global-scale search results are extremely low when the GNP number is small. Algorithm 3.1 shows the detailed algorithm description.

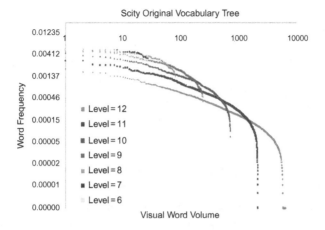

Figure 3.1 Visual word distribution in a 2-layer, 12-level vocabulary tree.

Algorithm 3.1 Greedy N-best Path algorithm.

---

1 **Input**: Query local interest point q tree depth $l = 1$.
2 Calculate the distances from the query point q to all k children nodes.
3 While($l < L$){
4 $l = l + 1$
5 The candidate set $=$ the N nearest children nodes in the depth $l - 1$.
6 Calculate the distances from the query point q to all kN candidates.
7 }
8 Return the index file of the nearest word.

Term Weighting Efficiency:
It is well-known that the *Zipf*'s Law[1] describes the distribution of textual words in documents in which the most frequent words account for a large portion of word occurrences. Due to the inappropriate hierarchical tree division, the visual word distribution does not follow the *Zipf*'s Law (Figure 2.8).

---

[1] http://en.wikipedia.org/wiki/Zipf's_law

Furthermore, with the increase in the hierarchical tree level, the word distribution becomes more and more uniform (Figure 3.1). Consequently, we can explain the phenomena observed in [32] that the IDF is less effective in large word volume. Subsequently, we can also infer that, in the current suboptimal hierarchical structure, the "stop words" removal technique won't be very helpful since there are not very many visual words in images like "*a*" or "*the*" in documents. Our inference is validated by the "stop words" removal experiments in [32].

Dictionary Generality across Different Databases

When retrieving a new database, a common strategy is to recluster a VT model and regenerate all BoW vectors. However, in many cases the computational cost of hierarchical reclustering is a large burden in a large-scale scenario. Hence, it is natural to want to reuse the original VT model in a new database. However, it is very hard to construct a generalized vocabulary tree and a generalized visual codebook that are suitable for any scenario, especially when the new database has different data volumes (e.g., 1K images vs. 1M images) and different image properties (e.g., images taken by mobile phones vs. images taken by specialized cameras). If we directly represent a new database by an old VT model, the differences in feature volumes and distributions would cause hierarchical unbalance and mismatches in middle levels, resulting in over-fitted BoW vectors at the leaf level. On the other hand, to maintain a retrieval system that is effective in retrieval tasks, one important extension to improve system flexibility is to maintain the retrieval system in a scalable and incremental scenario. In such a case, the regeneration of the retrieval model and reindexing of image contents are over cost. It would be much more reasonable and effective to enable the retrieval model to be adaptive to data variance by model updating and incremental learning.

3.2 DENSITY-BASED METRIC LEARNING

As shown above, the hierarchical structure will iteratively magnify the asymmetric quantization process in feature-space division, which resulted in suboptimal visual words and suboptimal IDF values in former papers [33] and [32]. To avoid this imbalance, we present a *density-based metric learning* (*DML*) algorithm: First, a *density field* is estimated in the original feature space (e.g., 128-dimensional SIFT space) to evaluate the distribution tightness of the local features. By extending denser clusters and shrinking sparser clusters, the similarity metric in k-means is modified to rectify the over-shorten or over-length quantization steps in hierarchical k-means. Subsequently, a refined VT is constructed by DML-based hierarchical k-means, which offers more "meaningful" tree nodes for retrieval.

3.2.1 Feature-Space Density-Field Estimation

To begin, we first introduce the definition of *density field*, which estimates the density of each SIFT point in the SIFT feature space as a discrete approximation. The density of a SIFT point in 128-dimensional SIFT feature space is defined by

$$D(i) = \frac{1}{n} \sum_{j=1}^{n} e^{-||x_i - x_j||_{L_2}}, \tag{3.1}$$

where $D(i)$ is the point density of the ith SIFT point, n is the total number of SIFT points in this dataset, and x_j is the jth SIFT point. We adopt $L2$ distance to evaluate the distance between two SIFT points.

To make it efficient, we resort to estimating the density of each SIFT point using only its local neighbors as an approximation as follows:

$$\tilde{D}(i, m) = \frac{1}{m} \sum_{k=1}^{m} e^{-||x_i - x_j||_{L_2}}, \tag{3.2}$$

where $\tilde{D}(i, m)$ is the point density of the ith SIFT feature in its m neighborhood. We only need to calculate the local neighbors of SIFT by: (1) Cluster database features into k clusters: $O(k * h * l)$, with h iterations to l points; and (2) nearest neighbor search in each cluster: $O(l2/k)$. By a large k (e.g., 2000), our DML would be very efficient. Using a heap structure, it could be even faster.

3.2.2 Learning a Metric for Quantization

From the above step, point-based density is estimated by neighborhood approximation. Subsequently, the similarity metric in hierarchical k-means are refined by density-based adaption as:

$$Similarity(c, i) = AveDen(c) \times Dis(C_{Center}, i). \tag{3.3}$$

$Similarity(c, i)$ is the similarity metric in DML-based k-means, which is the similarity between the cth cluster and the ith point; $AveDen(c)$ is the average density of the SIFT points in the cth cluster; and $Dis(c_{center}, i)$ is the distance between the center SIFT point of cluster c and the ith SIFT point.

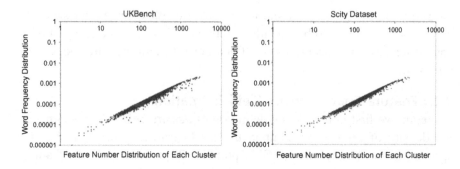

Figure 3.2 Feature-Frequency statistics (the scale of each axis is given by Log-Log).

We explain this operation as follows: From the viewpoint of information theory, the generation of a "visual word" would cause information loss in the hierarchical quantization process. In particular, hierarchical k-means quantizes the sparser points with larger steps than the denser points. Therefore, the information loss is much more severe in the "probable informative" points (less likely to appear in most images) than the "probable uninformative" points (more likely to appear in most images). The proposed DML method decreases the overall quantization error by shortening the quantization steps for sparser regions to represent the "meaningful" points more precisely. Similar to textual words, the sparser regions in the SIFT feature space could be analogized to more meaningful textual words while the denser regions could be compared to less meaningful textual words, or even "stop words". We demonstrate our inference by investigating the feature-word frequency in Figure 3.2. Our method can be also analogized to asymmetry quantization in signal processing.

To see how the DML-based method reduces the overall quantization error, we view the information loss of quantization using its weighted quantization error, in which the weight means the informative degree of the quantized word, which is evaluated by its IDF value. We denote the quantization error of the ith word as $QA(i)$ ($QA(i) > 0$):

$$QA(i) = \sum_{j=1}^{m_i} \sum_{k=1}^{128} (F_{ij}^{k\,2} - (\tilde{F}_i^k)^2), \qquad (3.4)$$

where F_{ji}^k is the kth feature dimension in the jth SIFT point of the ith cluster, $\tilde{F}_i^k$ is the kth feature dimension of the ith cluster center, m_i is the number of SIFT points in this cluster, and n is the number of words.

To evaluate the weighted quantization errors between the DML method and the original method, we compare their weighted signal-ratio rates as follows:

$$\frac{SNR_{DML}}{SNR_{Org}} = \frac{P_{Signal}^{DML}}{P_{Noise}^{DML}} \bigg/ \frac{P_{Signal}^{Org}}{P_{Noise}^{Org}} = \frac{\int x^2 p_x(x) dx}{\int [\Delta_{n_{DML}}(x)]^2 p_x(x) dx} \bigg/ \frac{\int x^2 p_x(x) dx}{\int [\Delta_{n_{Org}}(x)]^2 p_x(x) dx}$$

$$= \frac{\int [\Delta_{n_{Org}}(x)]^2 p_x(x) dx}{\int [\Delta_{n_{DML}}(x)]^2 p_x(x) dx}, \tag{3.5}$$

where w_i is the IDF of the ith cluster as its word weight and $p_x(x)$ and $\Delta_n(x)$ are the sampling probability and squared input-output difference of x, respectively. In its discrete case, Equation (3.5) can be replaced as Equation (3.6), in which we denote the DML case by superscript$'$ (such as n', j'', and $w_{i'}$):

$$\frac{SNR_{DML}}{SNR_{Org}} = \frac{\sum_{i=1}^{n} (w_i \sum_{j=1}^{m_i} \sum_{k=1}^{128} (F_{ij}^k - \tilde{F}_i^k)^2)}{\sum_{i'=1}^{n'} (w_i' \sum_{j'=1}^{m_{i'}} \sum_{k=1}^{128} (F_{i'j'}^k - \tilde{F}_{i'}^k)^2)} \tag{3.6}$$

$$Constrained\ by : \sum_{i=1}^{n} w_i = \sum_{i'=1}^{n'} w_{i'} \tag{3.7}$$

The above equation can be further rewritten as follows:

$$\frac{SNR_{DML}}{SNR_{Org}} = \frac{\sum_{k=1}^{128} \sum_{i=1}^{n} (w_i (\sum_{j=1}^{m_i} F_{ij}^{k2} - \sum_{j=1}^{m_i} 2F_{ij}^k \tilde{F}_i^k + m_i(\tilde{F}_i^k)^2))}{\sum_{k=1}^{128} A_{i'=1}^{n'} (w_{i'} (\sum_{j'=1}^{m_{i'}} F_{i'j'}^{k2} - \sum_{j'=1}^{m_{i'}} 2F_{i'j'}^k \tilde{F}_{i'}^k + m_{i'}(\tilde{F}_{i'}^k)^2))}$$

$$= \frac{\sum_{k=1}^{128} \sum_{i=1}^{n} (w_i (\sum_{j=1}^{m_i} F_{ij}^{k2} - 2m_i(\tilde{F}_i^k)^2 + m_i(\tilde{F}_i^k)^2))}{\sum_{k=1}^{128} \sum_{i'=1}^{n'} (w_{i'} (\sum_{j'=1}^{m_{i'}} F_{i'j'}^{k2} - 2m_{i'}(\tilde{F}_{i'}^k)^2 + m_{i'}(\tilde{F}_{i'}^k)^2))}$$

$$= \frac{(\sum_{i=1}^{n} (w_i \sum_{k=1}^{128} (\sum_{j=1}^{m_i} F_{ij}^{k2} - m_i(\tilde{F}_i^k)^2)))}{\sum_{i'=1}^{n'} (w_{i'} \sum_{k=1}^{128} (\sum_{j'=1}^{m_{i'}} (F_{i'j'}^k)^2 - m_{i'}(\tilde{F}_{i'}^k)^2)).} \tag{3.8}$$

The SIFT space is quantized into equal-numbered words, hence $n = n'$. Indeed, in Equation (3.8), $\sum_{k=1}^{128} (\sum_{j=1}^{m_i} F_{ij}^{k2} - m_i(\tilde{F}_i^k)^2)$ is the quantization error in the ith cluster with m_i points, identical to $QA(i)$. Therefore, Equation (3.8) can be viewed as:

$$\frac{SNR_{DML}}{SNR_{Org}} = \frac{\sum_{i=1}^{n}(w_i \sum_{j=1}^{m_i} \sum_{k=1}^{128}(F_{ij}^{k^2} - (\tilde{F}_i^k)^2))}{\sum_{i'=1}^{n}(w_{i'} \sum_{j'=1}^{m_{i'}} \sum_{k=1}^{128}(F_{i'j'}^{k}{}^2 - (\tilde{F}_{i'}^k)^2))}$$

$$= \frac{\sum_{i=1}^{n}(w_i QA(i))}{\sum_{i'=1}^{n'}(w_{i'} QA(i'))}. \tag{3.9}$$

Since denser regions appear in a larger portion of the images and hence would be assigned a very low IDF, it can be ignored in Equation (3.9), because its IDF is almost 0 due to the IDF's log-like nature. On the contrary, in the sparser region, the quantization step is much more finite compared to the original method. Such a region has a much larger IDF and contributes more to the weighted quantization error. Based on Equation (3.8), $QA(i)$ depends on: (1) point count m_i and (2) distance between each point j and its word center. By DML construction, in sparser regions, both (1) and (2) are smaller than they were in the original k-means, which leads to smaller quantization error $QA(i)$. In other words, our method quantizes "meaningful" regions with more finite steps, and "meaningless" regions with more coarse steps. Based on DML, we multiply the larger w with the smaller QA in Equation (3.9), while the larger QA corresponds to almost zero IDF weights. Evaluating the overall quantization error, it is straightforward that $\sum_{i=1}^{n}(w_i QA(i)) \geq \sum_{i'=1}^{n'}(w_{i'} QA(i'))$ and $SNR_{DML} \geq SNR_{Org}$. In other words, regardless of the quantization errors in meaningless words such as "a" and "the" (such words can be disregarded in similarity ranking as "stop words"), there are fewer weighted quantization errors in the DML-based tree.

3.3 CHAIN-STRUCTURE RECOGNITION

We further investigate how to better leverage such a model. We have found that the solutions for the (1) *hierarchical quantization error* and (2) *unbalance feature division* can be uniformly figured out by exploiting the DML-based tree hierarchy. This is because DML can address the unbalanced subspace division and the VT hierarchy itself contains the genesis of the quantization error.

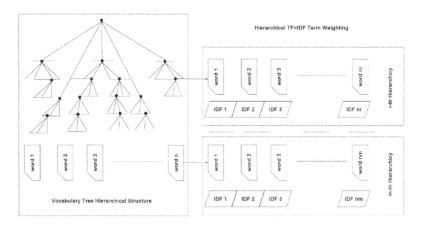

Figure 3.3 Hierarchical TF-IDF term weighting. Each hierarchial level is treated as a higher-level "visual word".

3.3.1 Chain Recognition in Dictionary Hierarchy

First, by expanding the TF-IDF term weighting procedure to hierarchical levels in the DML-based tree, the middle-level nodes are introduced into similarity ranking, which rectifies the magnified quantization errors in the leaves. In each hierarchical level, the IDF of the middle-node is calculated and recorded for middle-level matching. If the SIFT points are matched on a deeper level, their higher hierarchy would be hit by nature, meanwhile the ranking error of the leaf nodes caused by hierarchical quantization would be rectified in their higher hierarchy. Comparing to the *GNP* [27] method, our method offers an advantage in efficient computational cost, while maintaining comparable performance (see the subsequent Experimental section in this chapter).

Secondly, we have discovered that the integration of visual words in VT hierarchy is a natural analogy to boosting chain classification [84, 102], which brings us to a new perspective on [16] how to leverage tree hierarchy. (In [16], middle levels are simply combined as a unified weighted BoW vector in similarity ranking, which is similar to adopted pyramid matching for high-dimensional input data as a Mercer kernel for image categorization.) In a hierarchical tree structure, by treating each level as a classifier, the upper level has higher recall, while the lower level has higher precision. This is straightforward because the higher level represents the abstract of category representation and is more uniform, in which the similarity comparison is coarser. On the contrary, in the finest level, the features are very limited and

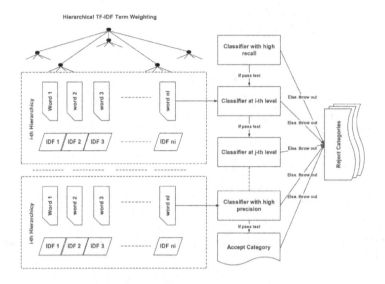

Figure 3.4 Hierarchical recognition chain by a vocabulary tree.

specified, leading to higher precision. In addition, the ranking results in each level being different due to their different quantization steps. Combining such hierarchical classifiers using a boosting chain manner can further improve retrieval.

As presented in Figure 3.4, each level is treated as an *"If...Else..."* classifier that discards the least confident categories out of a vertical-ordered boosting chain for multi-evidence similarity ranking. In implementation, SIFT points belonging to the same query image are parallel, put in this hierarchical recognition chain, level by level, to incrementally reject most categories, as presented in Algorithm 3.2:

For each retrieved scene or object, the overwhelming majority of samples available are negative. Consequently it is natural to adopt simple classifiers to reject most of the negatives and then use complex classifiers to classify the promising samples. In our proposed algorithm, the vocabulary tree is considered as a *hierarchical decision tree*, based on which the cascade decision process is made at each hierarchy. A positive result past the higher level triggers the evaluation of the deeper level. Compared with a boosting chain that usually adopts boosting feature selection, our method utilizes each hierarchical level as a "visual word" feature for rejection due to its coarse-to-fine inherence.

Algorithm 3.2 Vocabulary tree-based hierarchical recognition chain.

---

1 **Input:** Query image with m SIFT features, DML-constructed vocabulary tree with L level, ground-truth category set C: c_1-c_n; ascending rejection threshold K: k_1-k_l

2 **For** tree hierarchy i from 1 to L {

3 *If... Else...* **Test:** {

4 Go through each node n of ith level using query features;

5 Get the middle-level BoW query vector F_n of node n;

6 Compare F_n with BoW vectors of each category in C';

7 Discard top k_i dissimilar categories in C', updateC'; }

8 **Stop Test:** {

9 **If** category in C' is less than 1 {output the result}

10 **Else if** reach the finest level {rank remaining categories in C' and output the most similar category: c_{final}.} } }

11 **Output:** Hit category c_{final}

3.4 DICTIONARY TRANSFER LEARNING

Facing an incremental database, when the recognition system receives new image batches, it is natural to retrain the recognition model all over again. Although good performance can be expected, the computational cost would be extremely unacceptable once the database volume is very large. In particular, to maintain our system for an online service, such cost would not be acceptable.

The replacement of overall model retraining is that we only use a vocabulary tree to generate the BoW vectors for new images, without updating or retraining the VT-based recognition model. This is unrealistic, especially when there are new data patches coming.

Similar to the incremental case, we have discovered that the hierarchical tree structure can also facilitate the adaption of a VT-based retrieval model among different databases, which is important yet unexploited in literature. Different from reclustering the gigantic feature set of the new database, we present a novel tree adaption algorithm, *VT shift*, which enables: (1) adaption of the vocabulary tree among databases; and (2) incremental tree indexing in a dynamically updated database.

3.4.1 Cross-database Case

First, the SIFT features of the new database are sent through the original VT model, based on which the term weightings of the words are updated. The feature frequency of each leaf node reveals its rationality of existence and necessity of further expansion or removal. Leaf nodes that are either over-weighted or over-lightened would be adaptively re-assigned. Algorithm 3.2 presents our proposed VT shift algorithm.

Three operations are defined to iteratively refine the VT model to fit the new database:

1. *Leaf Delete:* If the feature frequency of a leaf is lower than a pre-defined minimum threshold, its features are reassigned back to its parent. Subsequently, this parent uses its sub-tree (with this parent as the root node) to assign the above features to their nearest leaves, except the deleted leaf.
2. *Parent Withdrawal:* If a leaf is the only child of its parent, and its feature frequency is lower than the minimum threshold, we withdraw this leaf and degrade its parent as a new leaf.
3. *Leaf Split:* If the feature frequency of a leaf is higher than the maximum threshold, we regrow this node into a sub-tree with the same branch factor in construction.

3.4.2 Incremental Transfer

We further leverage our proposed VT shift algorithm for incremental indexing in the *SCity* database. In our "Photo2Search" system-level implementation, we need a preliminary question about the genesis of new data. Algorithm 3.3 presents the details of the proposed VT Shift algorithm. Generally speaking, our system collects incremental scene images as well as their GPS locations from the three following sources:

1. Scene images uploaded by system administrators, which are directly sent into the database as a new data batch.
2. Query images sent by users to the server-end computer and images periodically crawled from *Flickr* API (we use both scene name and city name as crawling criterion), which are considered as *Under Evaluated*. For such data, pre-processing is conducted to further filter irrelevance: We treat each new image as a query example, for scene retrieval, if the *cosine* distance between this query and the best matched image is lower than T_{max} (i.e., they are similar enough), we add this image into the new data batch in our database.

To provide consistent service along with the process of incremental indexing, our system maintains two central computers on the server side. Each maintains a location recognition system that is set to be identical after finishing one round of adaption. Initially, the status of one system is set as *active* while the other as *inactive*. *Active* means this server program is now utilized to provide service; *inactive* means this server program is now utilized for incremental indexing. Once the *inactive* program receives a new batch of scene images, we first investigate whether it is necessary to activate the incremental indexing process. If so, we conduct incremental indexing and switch its *inactive* status to *active*, and vice versa; otherwise, these images are temporarily stored and added into subsequent new image batches.

Facing a new image batch, it is not always necessary to activate the incremental indexing process in the *inactive* server. If the distribution of the new data is almost identical to that of the original dataset, adaption could be postponed for the subsequent images. Hence, to reduce the computational cost in large data corpora, we conduct model adaption once either of following cases is true: (1) the volume of the new images is large enough or (2) the distribution of the new images is extremely diverse from that of the original database. We present an adaption trigger criterion using Kullback-Leibler (KL) diversity-based relative entropy estimation as in Figure 3.3 and explained in detail as follows.

First, data distribution is measured by its sample density, which is identical to the density field in DML-based tree construction. Facing a new data batch, we evaluate the data dissimilarity $Diver_{Accu}$ between the original database and the new data batch by their density-based KL-like relative entropy estimation:

$$Diver_{Accu} = \sum_{i=i}^{n} \tilde{D}_{new}(i, m) log \frac{\tilde{D}_{new}(i, m)}{\tilde{D}_{org}(Nearest(i), m)}, \quad (3.10)$$

in which $\tilde{D}_{new}(i, m)$ is the density of the new data at the ith data point in the mth neighborhood; $D_{org}(Nearest(i), m)$ is the density of the old data at the nearest old point of the ith new data in the mth neighborhood. It can be observed from the above equation that data diversity increases as: (1) the volume of the new data batch increases; (2) the distribution of the original database and new data batch are more diverse. Consequently, we control the incremental indexing process by trigger criterion as follows: When fusing a new data batch into the original database, the point density in

---

Algorithm 3.3 Dictionary transfer algorithm: VT Shift.

---

1 **Input:** SIFT feature set of new dataset.
2 **For** each feature in the new dataset {
3 Recalculate term weightings of words in new dataset; increase the hierarchical feature frequency *Fre* of each node that is in the path of current feature indexing }
4 Go through each leaf node n_i (with feature frequency Fre_i) of VT {
5 **If** $Fre_i \leq \xi_{min}$ or $Fre_i \geq \xi_{max}$ {Push n_i into the *Operation Array*.}}
6 **While** the *Operation Array* is not empty {Get the first element n_j
7 **If** $Fre_j \leq \xi_{min}$ {
8 **If** there are sibling leaves $n_j^{sibling}$ of this node{
9 *Leaf Delete*, push all sibling leaves (n_j^s) into *Operation Array*}
10 **Else** { *Parent Withdraw*, push n_j's parent as a renewed leaf into *Operation Array*}}
11 **If** $Fre_j \geq \xi_{min}$ {
12 *Leaf Split*, push new leaves $\{n_j^{split}\}$ into *Operation Array*}
13 Delete n_j}
14 **Output:** Refined vocabulary tree after adaption.

---

the original database need not be updated. Indeed, their former density estimations can be partially preserved and only need to be modified by new data (Algorithm 3.4):

$$\tilde{D}_{Update}(i, m) = \tilde{D}_{Org}(i, k) + \tilde{D}_{new}(i, m - k), \qquad (3.11)$$

where k is the number of remaining original points in m nearest neighbors, which is achieved by comparing the new data with the former-stored m nearest neighbors of each point.

3.5 EXPERIMENTS

In our experiments, two databases are investigated: *Scity* and *UKBench*. *Scity* consists of 20K street-side photos, captured along Seattle urban streets by a car automatically, as shown in Figures 3.5 and 3.6. We resized these photos to 400 × 300 pixels and extracted 300 features from each photo on average. Every six successive photos are grouped as a scene. The *UKBench* database contains 10K images with 2.5K objects (four images per category). We also leverage *UKBench* for performance evaluation, but not for scene

---

Algorithm 3.4 Visual dictionary transfer learning trigger detection.

---

1 **Input:** SIFT feature set of new dataset.

2 **For** each feature in the new dataset {

3 Recalculate term weightings of words in new dataset; increase the hierarchical feature frequency *Fre* of each node that is in the path of current feature indexing }

4 Go through each leaf node n_i (with feature frequency Fre_i) of VT {

5 **If** $Fre_i \leq \xi_{min}$ or $Fre_i \geq \xi_{max}$ {Push n_i into the *Operation Array*.}}

6 **While** the *Operation Array* is not empty {Get the first element n_j

7 **If** $Fre_j \leq \xi_{min}$ {

8 **If** there are sibling leaves $n_j^{sibling}$ of this node{

9 *Leaf Delete*, push all sibling leaves (n_j^s) into *Operation Array*}

10 **Else** { *Parent Withdraw*, push n_j's parent as a renewed leaf into *Operation Array*}}

11 **If** $Fre_j \geq \xi_{min}$ {

12 *Leaf Split*, push new leaves {n_j^{split}} into *Operation Array*}

13 Delete n_j}

14 **Output:** Refined vocabulary tree after adaption.

---

recognition task. In both databases, each category is divided into both a query set (test performance) and a ground truth set (create VT): In the *Scity* database, the last image of each scene is utilized for a query test while the former five images are adopted to construct the ground truth set. In the *UKBench* database (2.5K categories), the one image from each category is adopted to construct the query set while the rest are used to construct the ground truth set.

We use Success Rate at N (SR@N) to evaluate system performance. This measurement is commonly used in evaluating Question Answering (QA) systems. SR@N represents the probability of finding a correct answer within the top N results. Given n queries, SR@N is defined as Equation (3.10), in which d_q^j is the jth correct answer of the qth query, $pos(d_q^j)$ is its position, and $\Theta()$ is the Heaviside function: $\Theta(x) = 1$, if $x \geq 0$, and $\Theta(x) = 0$, otherwise.

$$SR@N = \frac{\sum_{q=1}^{n} \sum_{j=1}^{m_q} \Theta(N - pos(d_q^j))}{\sum_{q=1}^{n} m_q} \tag{3.12}$$

Figure 3.5 Exemplar photos in SCity database.

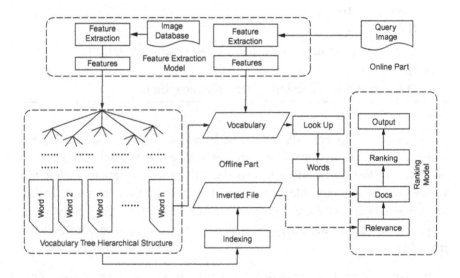

Figure 3.6 Vocabulary tree-based visual recognition model flowchart.

We build a 2-branch, 12-level vocabulary tree for both *Scity* and *UKBench*. The reason we leverage 2 divisions at each level is because of the consideration of large-scale application in real-world systems. With the same dictionary size, the search speed is with the log nature of branch number. For a VT with fixed word size (m), the search cost comparison of a-branch VT and b-branch VT for one SIFT point is $a\log_a(m)/b\log_b(m) = a\ln(b)/b\ln(a)$, which means the smaller branch factor results in much faster

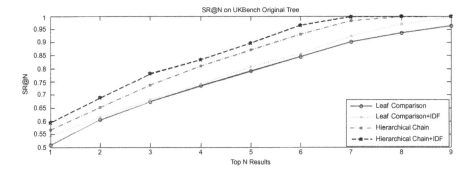

Figure 3.7 Performance comparison using original vocabulary tree in UKBench.

search speed. In both trees, if a node has less than 2,000 features, we stop its k-mean division, no matter whether it achieves the deepest level or not. In tree adaption, the maximum threshold ξ_{max} is set as 20,000; the minimum threshold ξ_{min} is set as 500.

3.5.1 Quantitative results

Figure 3.7 presents the SR@N in *UKBench* before and after DML, both of which conduct three comparisons: (1) leaf comparison, in which only leaf nodes are used in similarity ranking; (2) hierarchical chain, in which we adopt the hierarchical recognition chain for multi-evidence recognition; and (3) hierarchical chain + IDF, in which each level of the hierarchical recognition chain is combined with the IDF weights of their nodes in similarity ranking.

It is obvious that before DML learning, the real powers of the hierarchical recognition chain as well as the hierarchical IDF cannot be revealed well. But combinational performance enhancements of both methods after DML learning are significant, almost 20% over leaf-level baseline. Comparing Figure 3.7 with Figure 3.8, it is easy to see that the DML-based tree performs fairly better than the original tree, almost 20% enhancement to the best results. The same result holds in *Scity* as shown in Figures 3.9–3.10.

Indeed, this phenomenon can be expressed by Figure 3.11, after DML-based construction: the word distribution in the hierarchical level would follow *Zipf*'s Law better, which means not only middle-level nodes but also their IDF would be more discriminative and more meaningful.

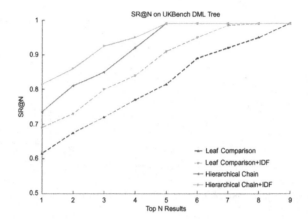

Figure 3.8 Performance comparison using DML-based vocabulary tree in UKBench.

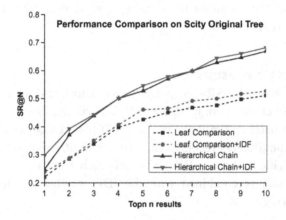

Figure 3.9 Performance comparison using original vocabulary tree in SCity.

Actually, without DML-based optimization, the hierarchical *k*-means would be biased to the denser regions and incorrectly divide them deeper and tighter rather than the sparse regions. This bias is hierarchically accumulated and wrongly assigns such regions with high IDF in recognition. This is why the use of IDF is not better in the original tree [30, 32], while it is better in the DML-based tree. Figure 3.12 further explains this enhancement in *UKBench*. On the left, the cluster diameter distribution in the 12th level is ranked by feature frequency. By DML construction, the diameter distribution is more uniform, so feature-space division is more uniform; on the right, quantization error distribution is ranked by image

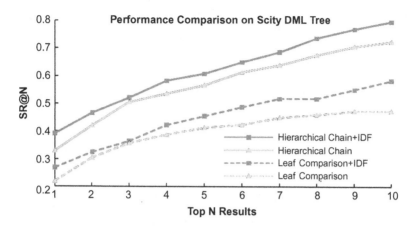

Figure 3.10 Performance comparison using DML-based vocabulary tree in SCity.

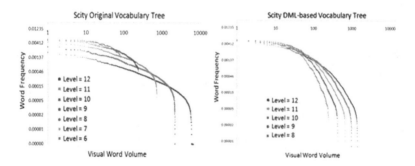

Figure 3.11 Visual words distribution in 1-way, 12-layer dictionary in SCity.

counts of clusters. The quantization errors with more images are higher, but in clusters with fewer images they are much lower. An intuitive motivation of DML-based tree construction is to refine the original distance metric in k-means clustering, which is achieved by generating more clusters in denser regions and less clusters in sparser regions. Since VT hierarchy magnifies unbalanced space division, DML revises such bias to rectify such unbalance.

We further investigate the efficiency of the hierarchical recognition chain. Figure 3.13 presents a comparison between our method and GNP [27]. We also evaluate how the chain level affects the recognition performance in *UKBench*. The method from Nister [16] that combines middle levels into a unified BoW vector is also given (Fig. 3.14). Compared to [16], the proposed method can achieve better performance. When $n > 14$,

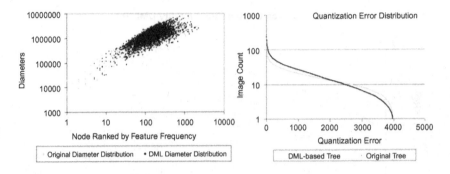

Figure 3.12 Visualized results of quantization error reduction.

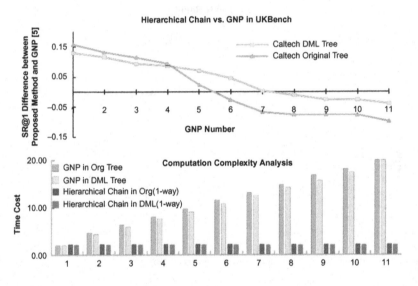

Figure 3.13 Precision and time comparison between hierarchical recognition chain (1-way) and GNP. (GNP number: 1-11).

performance begins to degenerate due to over-quantization. Compared to [16], VT has an advantage in efficient search in the large-scale case. Its cost is accuracy degeneration compared to solely SIFT matching. On the contrary, AKM in [10] merits in matching precision but it's time-consuming: (1) It use float k-means; and (2) to ensure precision, the k-d forest is also slow.

We evaluate our proposed *VT shift* algorithm with the following experiments: Figures 3.15–3.16 present the *VT shift* performance between *UKBench* and *Scity* with different volumes (9K vs. 20K) and applications

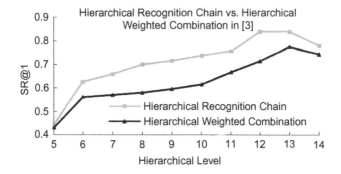

Figure 3.14 Performance of hierarchical chain at different hierarchy levels.

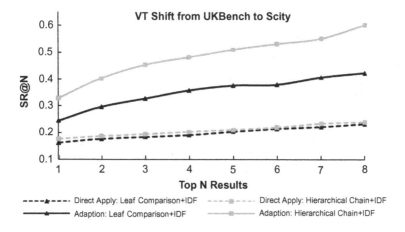

Figure 3.15 Performance of dictionary transfer learning from SCity to UKBench.

(scene vs. object). It is obvious that direct application of the dictionary across databases with different constitutions would cause severe performance degradation (Figure 3.17). However, the *VT shift* algorithm can well address the tree adaption problem. Table 3.2 presents the advantage of the DML-based tree in VT Shift operation over the original tree in both databases.

We further leverage our proposed VT shift algorithm for incremental indexing in the *SCity* database. In our "Photo2Search" system-level implementation, we should figure out a preliminary question about the genesis of

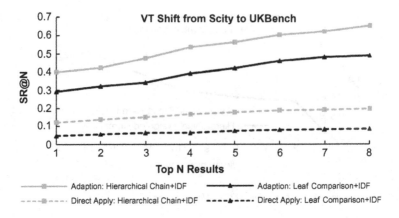

Figure 3.16 Dictionary transfer performance from UKBench to SCity.

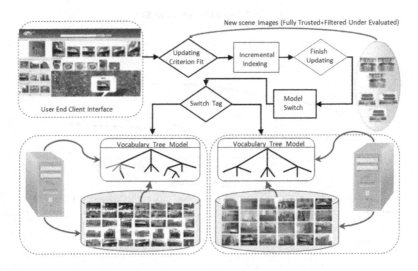

Figure 3.17 Recognition model updating.

new data (Figure 3.18). Generally speaking, our system collects incremental scene images as well as their GPS locations from the two following sources:

1. Scene images uploaded by system administrators, which are directly sent to the database as a new data batch.
2. Query images sent by users to the server-end computer and images periodically crawled from the *Flickr* API (we use both scene name and city name as crawling criterion), which are considered as *under evaluated*. For such data, pre-processing is conducted to further filter

Table 3.2 Performance analysis of VT Shift						
Reclustering (UKBench) vs. VT Shift (Scity-UKBench)						
Tree/SR@N	1	2	3	4	5	Time Cost
Org	0.20	0.29	0.38	0.43	0.50	8394.9s
DML	0.42	0.47	0.53	0.61	0.67	8279.5s
Shift Org	0.19	0.26	0.33	0.38	0.44	1937.4s
Shift DML	0.35	0.42	0.48	0.54	0.56	1988.2s
Reclustering (Scity) vs. VT Shift (Caltech101-Scity)						
Tree/SR@N	1	2	3	4	5	Time Cost
Org	0.15	0.27	0.34	0.40	0.43	6034.2s
DML	0.29	0.37	0.42	0.48	0.51	6129.4s
Shift Org	0.10	0.17	0.23	0.29	0.31	1434.7s
Shift DML	0.21	0.33	0.40	0.45	0.48	1125.3s

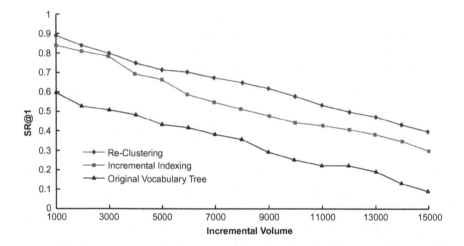

Figure 3.18 Sequential indexing without trigger criteria.

irrelevance: We treat each new image as a query example, for scene retrieval; if the *cosine* distance between this query and the best matched image is lower than T_{max} (i.e., they are similar enough), we add this image into a new data batch in our database.

To provide consistent service along with the process of incremental indexing, our system maintains two central computers on the server side. Each maintains a location recognition system that is set to be identical

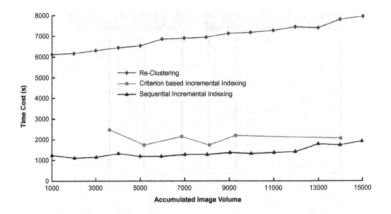

Figure 3.19 Time cost with/without trigger criteria.

after finishing one round of adaption. Initially, the status of one system is set as *active* while the other as *inactive*. *Active* means this server program is now utilized to provide service; *inactive* means this server program is now utilized for incremental indexing. Once the *inactive* program receives a new batch of scene images, we first investigate whether it is necessary to activate the incremental indexing process. If so, we conduct incremental indexing and switch its *inactive* status to *active* and vice versa; otherwise, these images are temporally stored and added into consequent new image batches.

Figure 3.19 presents the performance comparison between our proposed method and methods (1) and (2). With the increase of database volume, the SR@1 performance is naturally decreased. Although reclustering performs better than our proposed method, its time cost is unacceptable compared to both incremental indexing and simply using original VT to generate new BoW vectors. Our method can maintain comparable performance (less than 10% degradation than comparing to reclustering), while requiring fairly limited computational cost (24% cost compared to reclustering).

We compare our proposed incremental indexing with method 1), reclustering of an entire renewed database (it has the best performance as the performance upper limit and 2), original VT that only regenerates BoW vectors for new images. It has no adaption in tree structure and is the performance baseline. We not only compare their recognition performance using SR@1 (Figure 3.18) but also compare their adaption computation cost using their computational costs in Figure 3.20.

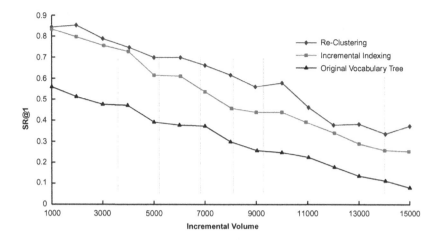

Figure 3.20 Incremental indexing with trigger criterion.

3.6 SUMMARY

This chapter demonstrated that exploiting the hierarchical structure of a vocabulary tree can largely benefit patch-based visual retrieval. We discovered that the hierarchical VT structure can allow us to (1) optimize visual dictionary generation; (2) reduce quantization errors in BoW representation; and (3) transfer the patch-based retrieval model across different databases. We presented a density-based metric learning (DML) algorithm to unsupervised optimize tree construction, which reduces both unbalanced feature division and quantization error. Subsequently, we introduced a hierarchical recognition chain to exploit middle levels to improve retrieval performance, which has an advantage in algorithm efficiency compared to *GNP* [5]. Compared to the–current retrieval baselines, our overall performance enhancement is 6–10% in the *UKBench* database and over 10-20% in the *Scity* scene database. Finally, we also discovered that the hierarchical tree structure can make the VT model reapplicable across different databases as well as adaptive to database variation to maintain considerable performance without reclustering. In our future work we will further investigate the influences of visual word synonymous and multivocal to improve retrieval efficiency.

CHAPTER 4

Supervised Dictionary Learning via Semantic Embedding

4.1 INTRODUCTION

In this chapter, our overall target is to embed the semantic labels into the building procedure of the visual dictionary. To this end, there are two main issues that should be taken into consideration. First, how do we obtain a precise correspondence set between local image patches and semantic labels? This is hard to achieve via manual patch annotations in large-scale applications. We subsequently resort to collaborative image tagging on the Web. Second, how do we model correlative semantic labels to supervise the building of a visual dictionary? Given a set of local features with (partial) semantic labels, this chapter introduces a hidden Markov random field to model the supervision from correlative semantic labels to local image patches. Our model consists of two layers: The observed field layer contains local features extracted from the entire image database, where the visual metric takes effect to quantize the feature space into codeword subregions. The hidden field layer models (partial) semantic labels with WordNet-based correlation constraints. Semantics in the hidden field follow the Markov property to produce Gibbs distribution over local features in the observed field, which gives generative supervision to jointly optimize the local feature quantization procedure. For more detailed innovations and experimental validations, please refer to our previous publication in IEEE International Conference on Computer Vision and Pattern Recognition 2010. The overall framework is outlined in Figure 4.1.

4.2 SEMANTIC LABELING PROPAGATION

To feed into the proposed semantic embedding algorithms, we need a set of correspondences from local feature patches to semantic labels. Each correspondence offers a unique label and a set of local features extracted

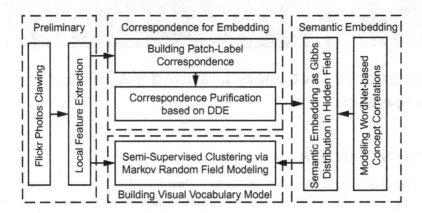

Figure 4.1 Semantic embedding framework.

from photos with this label. In the traditional approaches, such patch-label correspondences are collected by either manual annotations or from the entire training image. For the latter case, labeling noises are an unaddressed problem in large-scale scenarios.

To handle this problem, we present a Density Diversity Estimation (DDE) approach to purify the patch-label correspondences collected from Flickr photos with collaborative labels. As a case study, we collected over 60,000 photos with labels from Flickr. For each photo, difference of Gaussians salient regions are detected and described by SIFT [9]. Each correspondence contains a label and a set of SIFT patches extracted from Flickr photos with this label. We discard infrequent labels in WordNet that contains less than 10 photos in LabelMe [103]. The remaining correspondences are further purified to obtain a ground truth correspondence set [104] for semantic embedding. This set includes over 18 million local features with over 450,000 semantic labels, containing over 3,600 unique words.

4.2.1 Density Diversity Estimation
Given a label s_i, Equation (4.1) denotes its initial correspondence set as $< D_i, s_i >$, in which D_i denotes the set of local features $\{d_1, d_2, \ldots, d_{n_i}\}$ extracted from the Flickr photos with label s_i, and le_{ji} denotes a correspondence from label s_i to local patch d_j:

$$
\begin{aligned}
LE_i &= < D_i, s_i > \\
&= < \{d_1, d_2, \ldots, d_{n_i}\}, s_i >= \{le_{d_1 s_i}, \ldots, le_{d_{n_i} s_i}\}
\end{aligned}
\tag{4.1}
$$

The first criterion of our filtering is based on evaluating the distribution **density** in local feature space. For a given d_l, it reveals its representability for s_i. We apply nearest neighbor estimation in D_i to approximate the density of d_l in Equation (4.2):

$$Den_{d_l} = \frac{1}{m} \sum_{j=1}^{m} \exp(-||d_l - d_j||_{L2}), \tag{4.2}$$

where Den_{d_l} denotes the density for d_l, which is estimated from its m nearest local patch neighbors in the local feature space of D_i (for label s_i).

Another criterion of our filtering is based on evaluating the **diversity** of neighbors in d_l. It removes the dense regions that are caused by noisy patches from only a few photos (such as meshed photos with repetitive textures). We adopt neighbor uncertainty estimation based on the following entropy measurement. For the same reason, we apply nearest neighbor estimation in D_i to approximate the density of d_l in Equation (4.2):

$$Div_{d_l} = -\frac{n_j}{n_m} ln(\frac{n_j}{n_m}), \tag{4.3}$$

where Div_{d_l} represents the entropy at d_l, n_m is the number of photos that have patches within the m neighbors of d_l, and n_i is the total number of patches in photos with label s_i. Therefore, in local feature space, denser regions produced by a small fraction of the labeled photos will receive lower scores in our subsequent filtering in Equation (4.4).

Finally, we only retain the purified local image patches that satisfy the following DDE criterion:

$$D_i^{Purify} = \{d_j \,|\, DDE_{d_j} > T\} \quad s.t. \, DDE_{d_j} = Den_{d_j} \times Div_{d_j}. \tag{4.4}$$

To interpret the above formulation, for a given label s_i, DDE selects the patches that frequently and uniformly appear within photos annotated by s_i. After DDE purification, we treat the purified correspondence set as a ground truth to build correspondence links le_{ji} from semantic label s_i to each of its local patches d_j. Examples of the proposed DDE filtering is shown in Figure 4.2.

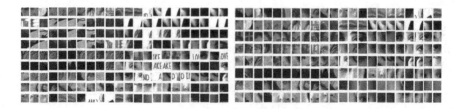

Figure 4.2 Original patch set (partial) and its DDE filtering for "Face".

4.3 SUPERVISED DICTIONARY LEARNING

4.3.1 Generative Modeling

We further present the proposed generative modeling for supervised dictionary learning. As shown in Figure 4.3, we introduce a hidden Markov random field (HMRF) model to integrate semantic supervision to quantize the local feature space. This model contains two layers:

- As the first layer, a *hidden field* contains a graph of correlative nodes $(S = \{s_i\}_{i=1}^{m})$. Each s_i denotes a unique semantic label, which provides correspondence links (le) to a subset of local features in the observed field. Another type of link l_{ij} between two given nodes s_i and s_j denotes their semantic correlation, which is measured by WordNet [105–107].
- As the second layer, an *Observed Field* contains local features ($D = \{d_i\}_{i=1}^{n}$) extracted from the image database. Similarity between the two nodes follows a visual metric. Once there is a link le_{ji} from d_i to s_j, we constrain d_i by s_j from the hidden field with conditional probability $P(d_i|s_j)$.

Hence, feature set D is regarded as (partial) generative from the hidden field, and each d_i is conditionally independent given S:

$$P(D|S) = \prod_{i=1}^{m}\{P(d_i|s_j) \mid P(d_i|s_j) \neq 0\}. \tag{4.5}$$

Here, we set a hard quantization case, i.e., to assign a unique cluster label c_i to each d_i. Therefore, D is quantized into a visual dictionary $\mathcal{W} = \{w_k\}_{k=1}^{K}$ (corresponding feature vectors $V = \{v_k\}_{k=1}^{K}$). The quantizer assignment for D is denoted as $C = \{c_i\}_{i=1}^{n}$. $c_i = c_j = w_k$ denotes d_i and d_j belongs to an identical visual word w_k. From Figure 4.3, the dictionary $\mathcal{W}$ and the semantics S are conditionally dependent given the observed field, which thereby incorporates S to optimize the building of $\mathcal{W}$.

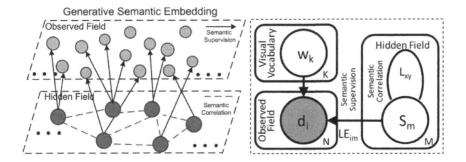

Figure 4.3 Semantic embedding by Markov Random Field.

In this chapter, we define a Markov random field on the hidden field, which imposes Markov probability distribution to supervise the quantizer assignments C of D in the observed field:

$$\forall i \quad P(c_i|C) = P(c_i \mid \{c_j \mid le_{jx} \neq 0, le_{iy} \neq 0, x \in \mathcal{N}'_y\}), \qquad (4.6)$$

Here, x and y are nodes in the hidden field that link to points i and j in the observed field, respectively (le_{jx} and $le_{iy} \neq 0$). $\mathcal{N}'_y$ is the hidden field neighborhood of y. The cluster label c_i depends on its neighborhood cluster labels ($\{c_j\}$). This "neighborhood" definition is within the hidden field (i.e., each c_j is the cluster assignment of d_j that has neighborhood labels (s_x) within $\mathcal{N}'_y$ for s_y of d_i).

Considering a particular configuration of quantizer assignments C (which gives a "visual dictionary" representation), its probability can be expressed as a Gibbs distribution [108] generated from the hidden field, depending on the following Hammersley-Clifford theorem [109]:

$$P(C) = \frac{1}{\mathcal{H}} \exp\left(-\mathcal{L}(C)\right) = \frac{1}{\mathcal{H}} \exp\left(-\sum_{k=1}^{K} \mathcal{L}_{\mathcal{N}_k}(w_k)\right), \qquad (4.7)$$

where $\mathcal{H}$ is a normalization constraint and $\mathcal{L}(C)$ is the overall potential function for the current quantizer assignment C, which can be decomposed into the sum of potential functions $\mathcal{L}_{\mathcal{N}_k}(w_k)$ for each visual word w_k, which only considers influences from points in w_k (volume $\mathcal{N}_k$).

To interpret the above calculation and formulation, let say two data points d_i and d_j in w_k contribute to $\mathcal{L}_{\mathcal{N}_k}(w_k)$ if and only if: (1) correspondence links

le_{xi} and le_{yj} exist from d_i and d_j to semantic nodes s_x and s_y, respectively; and (2) semantic correlation l_{xy} exists between s_x and s_y in the Hidden Field.

To solve it, we adopt the WordNet:Similarity [106] to measure l_{xy}, which is constrained to $[0, 1]$ with $l_{xx} = 1$. A large l_{xy} means a close semantic correlation (usually from correlative nouns, e.g., "rose" and "flower"). In Equation (4.8), we subtract the sum of l_{xy} to fit the potential function $\mathcal{L}(C)$. Intuitively, $P(C)$ gives higher probabilities to the quantizer that follows semantic constraints better. We calculate $P(C)$ by:

$$
\begin{aligned}
P(C) &= \frac{1}{\mathcal{H}} \exp\left(-\sum_{k=1}^{K} \mathcal{L}_{\mathcal{N}_k}(w_k)\right) \\
&= \frac{1}{\mathcal{H}} \exp\left(-\sum_{k=1}^{K} \sum_{i \in \mathcal{N}_k} \sum_{j \in \mathcal{N}_k} \left\{-l_{xy} \mid le_{xi} \neq 0 \wedge le_{yj} \neq 0\right\}\right).
\end{aligned}
\tag{4.8}
$$

4.3.2 Supervised Quantization

Overall, to achieve semantic embedding, we have $D = \{d_i\}_{i=1}^{n}$ in the observed field as generative from a particular quantizer configuration $C = \{c_i\}_{i=1}^{n}$ through its conditional probability distribution $P(D|C)$:

$$
P(D|C) = \sum_{i=1}^{n} P(d_i|c_i) = \sum_{i=1}^{n} \left\{P(d_i, v_k) \mid c_i = w_k\right\}.
\tag{4.9}
$$

Therefore, given c_i, the probability density $P(d_i, v_k)$ is measured by the visual similarity between feature point d_i and its visual word feature v_k. To obtain the best C, we investigate the overall posterior probability of a given C as $P(C|D) = P(D|C)P(C)$, in which we consider the probability of $P(D)$ as a constraint. Finding maximum-a-posterior of $P(C|D)$ can be converted to maximizing:

$$
\begin{aligned}
P(C|D) \propto P(D|C)P(C) \propto & \left(\sum_{i=1}^{n}\{P(d_i, v_k) \mid c_i = w_k\}\right) \\
& \times \left(\frac{1}{\mathcal{H}} \exp\left(\sum_{k=1}^{K} \sum_{i \in \mathcal{N}_k} \sum_{j \in \mathcal{N}_k} \{l_{xy} \mid le_{xi} \neq 0 \wedge le_{yj} \neq 0\}\right)\right).
\end{aligned}
\tag{4.10}
$$

Subsequently, two criteria are there to optimize the quantization configuration C (and hence the dictionary configuration $\mathcal{W}$): (1) The visual constraint $P(D|C)$ imposed by each point d_i to its corresponding word feature v_k, which is regarded as the quantization distortions of all visual words:

$$\sum_{i=1}^{n}\{P(d_i, v_k) \mid c_i = w_k\}$$

$$\propto \exp\left(-\sum_{i=1}^{n}\{Dis(d_i, v_k) \mid c_i = w_k\}\right); \tag{4.11}$$

and (2) The semantic constraints $P(C)$ imposed from the hidden field, which are measured as:

$$\frac{1}{\mathcal{H}} \exp\left(\sum_{k=1}^{K}\sum_{i\in\mathcal{N}_k}\sum_{j\in\mathcal{N}_k}\{l_{xy} \mid le_{xi} \neq 0 \wedge le_{yj} \neq 0\}\right). \tag{4.12}$$

It is worth noting that, due to the constraints in $P(C)$, MAP cannot be solved as a maximum likelihood. Furthermore, since the quantizer assignment C and the centroid feature vectors V could not be obtained simultaneously, we cannot directly optimize the quantization in Equation (4.10). We address this by a k-means clustering, which works in an estimation maximization manner to estimate the probability cluster membership. The E step updates the quantizer assignment C using the MAP estimation at the current iteration. Different from traditional k-means clustering, we integrate the correlations between data points by imposing $\frac{1}{\mathcal{H}} \exp\left(\sum_{k=1}^{K}\sum_{i\in\mathcal{N}_k}\sum_{j\in\mathcal{N}_k}\{l_{xy} \mid le_{xi} \neq 0 \wedge le_{yj} \neq 0\}\right)$ to select configuration C. The quantizer assignment for each d_i is performed in a random order, which assigns w_k to d_i and minimizes the contribution of d_i to the objective function. Therefore, $Obj(C|D) \triangleq \sum_{i=1}^{n} Obj(c_i|d_i)$. Without losing generality, we give a log estimation from Equation (4.10) to define the $Obj(c_i|d_i)$ for each d_i as follows:

$$Obj(c_i|d_i) = \arg\min_k(-Dis(d_i, v_k)$$

$$+\frac{1}{\mathcal{H}'}\sum_{j\in\mathcal{N}_k}\{l_{xy} \mid le_{xi} \neq 0 \wedge le_{yj} \neq 0\}) \tag{4.13}$$

The M step re-estimates the K cluster centroid vectors $\{v_k\}_{k=1}^{K}$ from the visual data assigned to them in the current E Step, which minimizes $Obj(c_i|d_i)$ in Equation (4.13) (equivalent to maximizing the expects of "visual words"). We update the kth centroid vector v_k based on the visual data within w_k:

$$v_k = \frac{\sum_{d_i \in W_k} d_i}{||W_k||} \quad s.t. \quad W_k = \{d_i | c_i = w_k\}. \tag{4.14}$$

Single-Level Dictionary: Algorithm 4.1 presents the building flow of a single-level dictionary. Our time cost is almost identical to the traditional k-means clustering. The only additional cost is the nearest neighbor calculation in the hidden field for $P(C)$, which can be performed using an $o(m^2)$ sequential scanning for m semantic labels (each with a heap ranking) and stored beforehand.

Hierarchical Dictionary: Many large-scale retrieval applications usually involve tens of thousands of images. To ensure online search efficiency, hierarchical quantization is usually adopted, e.g., vocabulary tree (VT) [16], approximate k-means (AKM) [24], and their variations. We also deploy our semantic embedding to a hierarchical version, in which the vocabulary tree model [16] is adopted to build a visual dictionary based on hierarchical

---

Algorithm 4.1 Building a Supervised Visual Dictionary.

---

1 **Input**: Visual data $D = \{d_i\}_{i=1}^n$, Semantic supervision $S = \{s_j\}_{j=1}^m$, Correspondence set $\{LE_1, \ldots, LE_m\}$, and Semantic correlation l_{ij} for any two s_i and s_j calculated by WordNet::Similarity [106], Maximum iteration N_I.

2 **Pre-computing**: Calculate the nearest neighbors in the hidden field using an $o(m^2)$ sequential scanning heap. Initialize a random set of clustering centers $W = \{w_k\}_{k=1}^K$.

3 **Iterative EM Steps:while** $\{V = \{v_k\}_{k=1}^K$ *still changes or the number of iterations is within N_I}* **do**

4   **E Step**: For each d_i in D, assign $c_i = w_k$ that satisfies the objective function in Equation (4.13), in which nearest neighbors in the hidden field are obtained from pre-computing (Step 2).

5   **M Step**: For each w_k in W, update its corresponding feature vector v_k based on Equation (4.14).

6 **end**

7 **Output::** Supervised dictionary $C = \{c_k\}_{k=1}^K$ with its inverted indexing structure (Indexed after EM).

---

k-means clustering. Compared to single-level quantization, the vocabulary tree model pays extreme attention on the search efficiency: To produce a bag-of-words vector for an image using a w-branch m-word VT model, the time cost is $O(w \log(w(m)))$, whereas using a single-level word division, the time cost is $O(m)$. During hierarchical clustering, our semantic embedding is identical within each subcluster.

4.4 EXPERIMENTS

We give two groups of quantitative comparisons in our experiments. The first group shows the advantages of our generative semantic embedding (GSE) to the unsupervised dictionary construction schemes, including comparisons to (1) the traditional VT [16] and GNP, and (2) the GSE without semantic correlations (ignoring semantic links in the hidden field graph to infer $P(C)$). The second group compares our GSE model with two related works in building a supervised dictionary for object recognition tasks: (1) Class-specific adaptive dictionary [42], and (2) learning-based visual word merging [110]. During comparison, we also investigate how the *dictionary sparsity*, *embedding strength*, and *label noise* (these concepts will be explained later) affect our performance.

4.4.1 Database and Evaluations

In this chapter, two databases are adopted in evaluation: (1) The Flickr database contains over 60,000 collaboratively labeled photos, which gives a real-world evaluation for our first group of experiments. It includes over 18 million local features with over 450,000 user labels (over 3,600 unique keywords). For Flickr, we randomly select 2,000 photos to form a query set, and use the remaining 58,000 to build our search model. (2) The PASCAL VOC 05 database [111] evaluates our second group of experiments. We adopt VOC 05 instead of 08 since the former directly gives quantitative comparisons to [110], which is most related to our work. We split PASCAL into two equal-sized sets for training and testing, which is identical to the settlement in [110]. The PASCAL training set provides bounding boxes for image regions with annotations, which naturally gives us the purified patch-label correspondences.

4.4.2 Quantitative Results

In the Flickr database, we build a 10-branch, 4-level vocabulary tree for semantic embedding, based on the SIFT features extracted from the entire database. If a node has fewer than 2,000 features, we stop its k-means division, whether it has achieved the deepest level or not. A document list (approximately 10,000 words) is built for each word to record which photo contains this word, thus forming an inverted index file. In the online processing, each SIFT feature extracted from the query image is sent to its nearest visual word, in which the indexed images are picked out to rank the similarity scores to the query. As a baseline approach, we build a 10-branch, 4-level unsupervised vocabulary tree for the Flickr database. The same implementations are carried out for the PASCAL database, in which we reduce the number of hierarchical layers to 3 to produce a visual dictionary with visual word volume $\approx 1,000$.

Similar to [42], it is informative to look at how our semantic embedding affects the averaged ratios between inter-class and intra-class distances. The inter-class distance is the distance between two averaged BoW vectors: one from photos with the measured semantic label, and one from random-select photos without this label; the intra-class distance is the distance between two BoW vectors from photos with an identical label. Our embedding ensures that nearby patches with identical or correlative labels would be more likely to quantize into an identical visual word. In Figure 4.4, this distance ratio would significantly increase after semantic embedding.

Figure 4.5 shows our semantic embedding performances in the Flickr database, with comparisons to both VT [16] and GNP [27]. With identical dictionary volumes, our GSE model produces a more effective dictionary than VT. Our search efficiency is identical to VT and much faster than GNP. In the dictionary building phase, the only additional cost comes from calculating $P(C)$. Furthermore, we also observe that a sparse

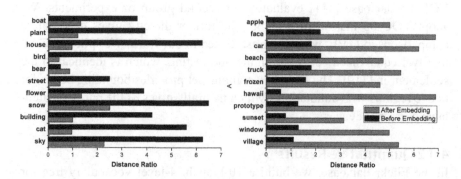

Figure 4.4 Ratios between inter-class distance and intra-class distance with and without semantic embedding.

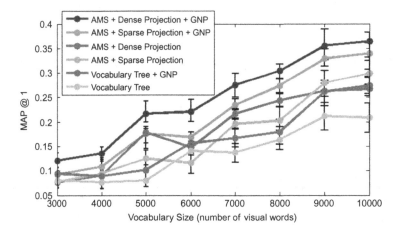

Figure 4.5 MAP comparisons between GSE and VT, GNP in Flickr.

dictionary (with fewer features per visual word on average) gives generally better performance by embedding an identical amount of patch-label correspondences.

We explore semantic embedding with different correspondence sets constructed by (1) different label noise T (DDE purification strength) (original strength t is obtained by cross-validation) and (2) different embedding strength S ($S = 1.0$ means we embed the entire purified correspondence set to supervise the codebook, 0.5 means we embed half). There are four groups of experiments in Figure 4.6 used to validate our embedding effectiveness: (a) GSE (without hidden field correlations Cr.) + Varied T, S: It shows that uncorrelative semantic embedding does not significantly enhance MAP by increasing S (embedding strength), and degenerates dramatically with large T (label noise), mainly because the semantic embedding improvement is counteracted by miscellaneous semantic correlations. (b) GSE (without hidden field correlations Cr.) + Varied T, S + GNP: Employing GNP could improve MAP performance to a certain degree. However, the computational cost would be increased. (c) GSE (with Cr.) + Varied T, S: Embedding with correlation modeling is a much better choice. Furthermore, the MAP degeneration caused by large T could be refined by increasing S in large-scale scenarios. (d) GSE (With Cr.) + Varied T, S + GNP: We integrate the GNP in addition to GSE to achieve the best MAP performance among methods (a)–(d). However, its online search is time-consuming due to GNP (Figure 4.7).

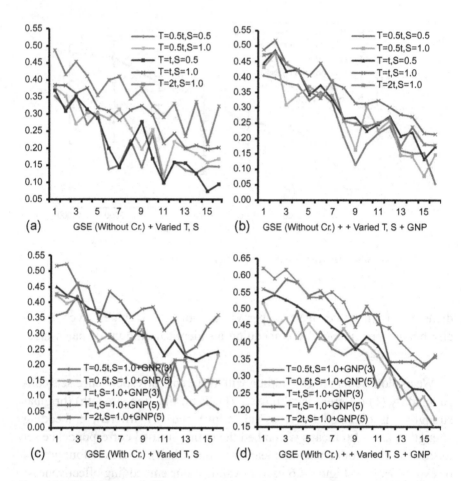

Figure 4.6 MAP with different embedding cases.

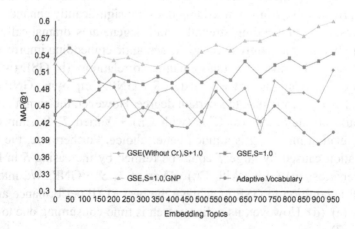

Figure 4.7 Comparison with adaptive dictionary in Flickr 60,000.

We compare our supervised dictionary with two learning-based vocabularies in [42, 110]. First, we show comparisons between our GSE model and the adaptive dictionary [42] in the Flickr database. We employed the nearest neighbor classifier in [110] for both approaches, which reported the best performance among alternative approaches in [110]. For [42], the nearest neighbor classification is adopted to each class-specific dictionary. It votes for the nearest BoW vector, assigning its label as a classification result. Not surprisingly, within limited (tens of) classes, the adaptive dictionary [42] outperforms our approach. However, putting more labels into dictionary construction will increase our search MAP. Our method can finally outperform the adaptive dictionary [42] when the number of embedding labels is larger than 171. In addition, adding new classes into the retrieval task would linearly increase the time complexity of [42]. In contrast, our search time is constant without regard to embedding labels. Second, we also compare our approach to [110] within the PASCAL VOC. We built the correspondence set based on the SIFT features extracted from the bounding boxes with annotation labels [111], from which we conducted the semantic embedding with $S = 1.0$. In classifier learning, each annotation is viewed as a class with a set of BoW vectors extracted from the bounding box with this annotation. Identical to [110], the classification of the test bounding box (we know its label beforehand as ground truth) is a nearest neighbor search process. Figure 4.8 shows that, in almost all categories, our method gives better precision than [110] within ten identical PASCAL categories.

True Label	Inferred Label								
	Build.	Grass	Tree	Cow	Sky	Aerop.	Face	Car	Bicyc.
Build.	38			2	1		1	2	1
Grass		66	1						
Tree	1	1	30						1
Cow				21			2		
Sky					46				
Aerop.	4					11			
Face							15		
Car								15	
Bicyc.	1								14

True Label	Inferred Label								
	Build.	Grass	Tree	Cow	Sky	Aerop.	Face	Car	Bicyc.
Build.	43		1					1	
Grass		66	1						
Tree		2	31						
Cow				23					
Sky		1			45				
Aerop.	2					13			
Face							15		
Car								14	1
Bicyc.									15

Figure 4.8 Confusion tables on PASCAL VOC 05 with comparison to Universal Vocabulary Confusion tables on PASCAL VOC 05 in comparison to universal dictionary.

4.5 SUMMARY

This chapter presented a semantic embedding framework, which aims for supervised, patch-based visual representation from collaborative Flickr photos and labels. Our framework introduced a hidden Markov random field to generatively model the relationships between correlative Flickr labels and local image patches to build supervised dictionary. By simplifying the Markov properties in the hidden field, we showed that both unsupervised and supervised quantizations (without considering semantic correlations) can be derived from our model. In addition, we have published a patch-label correspondence set [104] (containing over 3,600 unique labels with over 18 million patches) to facilitate subsequent research of this topic.

One interesting issue remains open: For large-scale applications, the generality of the supervised dictionary needs further exploration. Transfer learning is a feasible solution to adapt a supervised dictionary among different scenarios, e.g., from scene recognition to object detection, which will be further considered in our future work. The related works based on this chapter were accepted as oral presentations in IEEE CVPR 2010, as well as in *IEEE Transactions on Image Processing*.

CHAPTER 5

Visual Pattern Mining

5.1 INTRODUCTION

Most existing scalable visual search systems are built based upon visual vocabulary models with inverted indexing structures [16, 24, 27, 30]. In such a case, the local features extracted from a reference image are quantized into visual words, whose ensemble constitutes a bag-of-words histogram and the image is inverted indexed into every nonzero words correspondingly. This bag-of-words representation offers sufficient robustness against photographing variances in occlusions, viewpoints, illuminations, scales, and backgrounds. And the image search problem is transferred into a document retrieval problem, where several well-used techniques like TF-IDF [28], pLSA [117], and LDA [78] can be further deployed.

Motivation. Although bag-of-words representation well handles the photographic variances, one significant drawback comes from ignoring the spatial layouts of words. To a certain degree, this can be compensated by predefined spatial embedding strategies to group neighborhood words, for instance feature bundling [75] and max/min pooling [118]. Or alternatively, a more time-consuming solution is to carry out spatial verification, such as RANdom SAmple Consensus (RANSAC) and neighborhood voting [30].

Nevertheless, the discriminability of pairing or grouping words within each image are *not alone*, but in turn highly depends on the overall spatial layout statistics of word combinations in the reference image collection. To this end, rather than designing the spatial embedding for individual images independently [75, 118], a more *data driven* alternative is to discover such discriminative pairing or grouping of visual words from the image corpus. This is referred as "visual patterns" or "visual phrases" [69–72] as from the information retrieval literature, and typically involves techniques like colocation mining [99].

More formally speaking, a visual pattern is a meaningful spatial combination of visual words, which can be regarded as a semifully geometrical dependency model, where the geometry of each part depends only on its neighbors. Comparing to previous works in class-driven spatial modeling where restrictive priors and parameters are demanded [67, 119], visual patterns have been well advocated by their parameter-free intrinsic, i.e., all structures within visual patterns are obtained by data mining with class or category supervision. This intrinsic is of fundamental importance for the scalability, which on the opposite is the key restriction for the previous works [67, 119].

Problem. Two important problems are left open in the existing visual pattern mining paradigm:

- The existing visual patterns are built on the 2D word concurrences within individual images. It suffers from the ill-posed 2D photographic degeneration to capture their real-world 3D layouts. For instance words from different depth or different foreground/background objects can be nearby under certain 2D perspectives, but such spatial concurrence is not robust and discriminative enough with un controlled viewpoint variations. Figure 5.1 shows several examples of these incorrect configurations.
- Given the mined patterns, how to design a compact yet discriminative image representation is left unexploited in the literature. To this end, visual patterns are typically treated as compensative dimensions appended the bag-of-words histogram [69–72], which simply follows the standard usage of textual patterns in the traditional document retrieval endeavor. We argue that the purely pattern-level representation can be also discriminative enough, given a well-design pattern selection approach as in Section 5.2.1.[1] This pattern-level compact descriptor well suits for several emerging applications like low bit rate mobile visual search [120], as detailed in Section 5.4.

Figure 5.1 Exemplar illustrations of incorrect 2D neighborhood configurations of visual words, which are caused by either binding words with diverse depth, or binding words from both foreground and background objects, respectively.

---

[1]This argument contradicts to the traditional document retrieval endeavor, where textual patterns are typically attached as additional dimensions to the bag-of-words-based vector space model. One explanation is that the visual word dependency has a clear spatial structure, which is more discriminative comparing to the contextual concurrence of textual words.

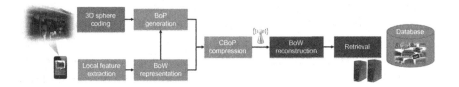

Figure 5.2 The proposed compact bag of patterns (CBoP) descriptor with application to low bit rate mobile visual search.

Approach. We propose a compact bag-of-patterns (CBoP) descriptor to address both issues toward a compact yet discriminative image representation. Figure 5.2 outlines the workflow of our CBoP descriptor, which is built based upon the popular bag-of-words representation. In preliminary, we assume that each target (e.g., object or landmark instance) in the dataset contains multiple reference images captured at different viewing angles. Using these images, a 3D point cloud is built for this target by structure-from-motion [121]. Then, we present a 3D sphere coding scheme to construct the initial pattern candidates, which eliminates the ill-posed 2D spatial layout in individual images by binding visual word concurrence within their 3D point cloud.

In visual pattern mining, we introduce a *"gravity distance"* to measure the closeness between two words to better captures their relative importance. This "gravity" incorporates the mutual information between the frequencies (or so-called *saliencies*) of both words into the subsequent *a priori*-based frequent itemset mining [122] procedure.

The mined patterns are further pooled together to build a CBoP histogram. This pooling operation seeks an optimal tradeoff between the descriptor compactness and its discriminability, which is achieved by sparse coding to minimize the number of selected patterns, typically at hundreds of bits, under a given distortion between the resulted CBoP histogram and the originally bag-of-words histogram. Finally, supervised labels can be also incorporated into the above formulation to further improve the performance.

Application. The mined CBoP descriptor has potentials in multidisciplinary applications such as object recognition, visual search, and image classification. In this paper, we demonstrate its usage in the emerging *low bit rate mobile visual search* application, where visual descriptors are directly extracted and sent instead of the query image to reduce the query delivery latency in mobile visual search [112, 113, 120]. In such a scenario, the extracted descriptor is expected to be compact, discriminative, and computationally efficient. While most state-of-the-art works target at abstracting or compressing the high-dimensional bag-of-words histogram [112, 120], the pattern-level abstraction is a natural choice but left unexploited in the literature. We provide two additional arguments to support such patter-level descriptor:

- First, previous works are deployed based on the linear combination of visual words for instance boosting [120], which selects one word in each round into the compact descriptor. It is a natural extension to look at their higher-oder combinations, i.e., patterns, to further improve the compression rate.
- Second, we argue that a pattern-level descriptor benefits in both memory cost and extraction time, i.e., only word combination/selection operations over the initial bag-of-words histogram, which is memory light and almost real-time comparing to other alternatives like topic features [114, 115, 123].

In practice, our CBoP has achieved almost identical search accuracy comparing to the million scale bag-of-words histogram, with an approximate 100-bit descriptor size. This performance significantly beats the state-of-the-art alternatives like 2D visual patterns [71, 72], topic features [114, 115, 123], and Hashing-based descriptors [116].

Outline. The rest of this chapter is organized as follows: Section 5.2 introduces our discriminative 3D visual pattern mining and CBoP extraction scheme. Section 5.3 shows its application in the low bit rate mobile landmark search prototype, and Section 5.4 details quantitative comparisons to the state-of-the-art works [16, 71, 72, 114–116]. For more details of this chapter, please refer to our publication in IEEE Transactions on Image Processing (2013).

5.2 DISCRIMINATIVE 3D PATTERN MINING

In this section, the proposed CBoP descriptor generation is presented. Our 3D pattern mining and CBoP descriptor construction are deployed based on the bag-of-words image representation. Suppose we have M target of interest (ToI) in total, each of which could be an object instance, a scene, a landmark, or a product. For each ToI, we also have a set of reference images captured from different viewpoints. For the sake of generality, we assume these reference images do not have tags to identify the viewing angles, e.g., inter- and intracamera parameters.[2] For each ToI, we first introduce a 3D sphere coding scheme to build the initial pattern candidate collection, following by a novel gravity distance-based pattern mining algorithm in Section 5.2.1. Finally, patterns from individual ToIs are pooled together to extract the CBoP histogram as detailed in Section 5.2.2.

5.2.1 The Proposed Mining Scheme

3D sphere coding. Formally speaking, for each reference image I_i ($i \in [1, n_t]$) of the tth ToI ($t \in [1, M]$), suppose there are J local descriptors $\mathbf{L}(i) = [L_1(i), \ldots, L_J(i)]$ extracted from I_i, which is quantized into an m-dimensional bag-of-words histogram $\mathbf{V}(i) = [V_1(i), \ldots, V_m(i)]$. We denote the spatial positions of $\mathbf{L}(i)$ as $\mathbf{S}(i) = [S_1(i), \ldots, S_J(i)]$, where each $S_j(i)$ ($j \in [1, J]$) is the 2D or 3D spatial position of the jth local descriptor. For each $S_j(i)$, we scan its spatial k-nearest neighborhood to identify all concurrent words

$$\mathbf{T}_j(i) = \left\{ L_{j'}(i) | L_{j'}(i) \in \mathbf{L}(i), \ S_{j'}(i) \in kNN\big(S_j(i)\big) \right\} \tag{5.1}$$

where $\mathbf{T}_j(i)$ (if any) is called an "transaction" built for $S_j(i)$ in I_i. We denote all transactions in I_i with order K as:

$$\mathbf{T}^k(i) = \left\{ \mathbf{T}_j(i) \right\}_{j \in [1, J]} \tag{5.2}$$

All k-order transactions found for images $[I_1, \ldots, I_{n_t}]$ in the tth ToI is defined as $\mathbf{T}^k(\text{ToI}_t) = \{\mathbf{T}^k(1), \ldots, \mathbf{T}^k(n_t)\}$. The goal of pattern mining is to mine n_t patterns from $\{\mathbf{T}^k(\text{ToI}_t)\}_{k=1}^K$, i.e., $\mathbf{P}_t = \{P_1, \ldots, P_{n_t}\}$ form each tth ToI and ensemble them together as $\{\mathbf{P}_t\}_{t=1}^M$.[3]

While the traditional pattern candidates are built based on the coding the 2D concurrences of visual words within individual reference images, we propose to search the k-nearest neighbors in the 3D point cloud of each tth ToI. Such a point cloud is constructed by structure-from-motion over the reference images with bundle adjustment [121]. Figure 5.3 shows several 3D

---

[2]Different from the previous works in supervised pattern mining, we build the initial pattern candidates from images of the same object instance, rather than from the same target category. But our subsequent pattern mining approach in Section 5.2.1 is also general for 2D pattern configurations from images of identical category

[3]Note that the k-nearest neighbor could be either 2D or 3D, either of which will be reformulated later by a *gravity* distance metric.

Figure 5.3 Visualized examples about the point clouds for visual pattern candidate construction. Exemplar landmark locations are within Peking University.

sphere coding examples in the 3D point clouds of representative landmarks as detailed in Section 5.4.

Distance-based pattern mining. Previous works in visual pattern mining mainly resort to **Transaction-based Colocation pattern Mining (TCM)**. For instance, works in [69–71] built transaction features by coding the k-nearest words in 2D.[4] A transaction in TCM can be defined by coding the 2D spatial layouts of neighborhood words. Then frequent itemset mining algorithms like *a Priori* [122] are deployed to discover meaningful word combinations as patterns, which typically check the pattern candidates from orders 1 to K.

TCM can be formulated as follows: Let $\{V_1, V_2, \ldots, V_m\}$ be the set of all potential items, each of which corresponds to a visual word in our case. Let $\mathbf{D} = \{\mathbf{T}_1, \mathbf{T}_2, \ldots, \mathbf{T}_n\}$ be all possible transactions extracted as above, each is a possible combination of several items within $\mathbf{V}$ after spatial coding. Here for simplification, we use $i \in [1, n]$ to denote all transactions discovered with orders 1 to K and in ToIs 1 to M. Let $\mathbf{A}$ be an "itemset" for the a given transaction $\mathbf{T}$, we define the support of an itemset as

$$\text{support}(\mathbf{A}) = \frac{|\{\mathbf{T} \in \mathbf{D} | \mathbf{A} \subseteq \mathbf{T}\}|}{|\mathbf{D}|}, \tag{5.3}$$

---

[4]This spatial configuration can be further refined by incorporating the scales of interest points, which imposes scale invariance into transactions [72].

If and only if support(**A**) $\geq s$, the itemset **A** is defined as a frequent itemset of **D**, where s is the threshold to restrict the minimal support rate. Note that any two $\mathbf{T}_i$ and $\mathbf{T}_j$ are induplicated.

We then define the confidence of each frequent itemset as:

$$
\begin{aligned}
\text{condifence}(\mathbf{A} \to \mathbf{B}) &= \frac{\text{support}(\mathbf{A} \cup \mathbf{B})}{\text{support}(\mathbf{A})} \\
&= \frac{|\{\mathbf{T} \in \mathbf{D} | (\mathbf{A} \cup \mathbf{B}) \subseteq \mathbf{T}\}|}{|\{\mathbf{T} \in \mathbf{D} | \mathbf{A} \subseteq \mathbf{T}\}|},
\end{aligned}
\tag{5.4}
$$

where **A** and **B** are two itemsets. The confidence in Equation (5.4) is defined as the maximal likelihood that **B** is correct in the case that **A** is also correct. Confidence-based restriction is to guarantee that the found patterns can discover the minimal item subsets, which are most helpful in representing the visual features at order $k \in [2, K]$.

To give a minimal association hyperplane to bound **A**, an *Association Hyperedge* of each **A** is defined as:

$$
AH(\mathbf{A}) = \frac{1}{N}\text{confidence}\left((\mathbf{A} - \{V_i\}) \to V_i\right).
\tag{5.5}
$$

Finally, by checking all possible itemset combinations in **D** from order 2 to K, the itemsets with support() $\geq s$ and $AH \geq \gamma$ are defined as frequent patterns.

One crucial issue lies in TCM would generate repeated patterns in texture regions containing dense words. To address this issue, distance-based Colocation pattern mining (**DCM**) is proposed with two new measures named participation ratio (pr) and participation index (pi).

First, a *R-reachable* measure is introduced as the basis of both pi and pr: Two words V_i and V_j are R-reachable when

$$
\text{dis}(V_i, V_j) < d_{\text{thres}},
\tag{5.6}
$$

where dis() is the distance metric such as Euclidean and d_{thres} is the distance threshold. Subsequently, for a given word V_i, we define its partition rate pr($\mathbf{V}, V_i$) as the percentage of subset $\mathbf{V} - \{V_i\}$ that are R-reachable:

$$
\text{pr}(\mathbf{V}, V_i) = \pi \frac{\left(\big|\text{instance}(\mathbf{V})\big|\right)}{\big|\text{instance}(V_i)\big|},
\tag{5.7}
$$

where π is the relational projection operation with deduplication. The participation index pi is defined as:

$$pi(\mathbf{V}, V_i) = \min_{i=1}^{m}\{pr(\mathbf{V}, V_i)\}, \tag{5.8}$$

where pi describes the frequency of subset $\mathbf{V} - V_i$ in the neighborhood. Note that only item subsets with pi larger than a give threshold is defined as patterns in **DCM**.

Gravity distance R-reachable: In many cases, the Euclidean distance cannot discriminatively describe the colocation visual patterns, which is due to it ignores the word discriminability and scale in building items. Intuitively, words from the same scale tend to share more commonsense in building items, and more discriminative words also produce more meaningful items. We then proposed a novel *gravity distance R-reachable* (*GD R-reachable*) to incorporate both cues. Two words V_i and V_j are GD R-reachable once $R_{i,j} < Cr_ir_j$ in the traditional **DCM** model, where r_i and r_j are the local feature scales of V_i and V_j, respectively, C is the fixed parameter, and $R_{i,j} = dis(V_i, V_j)$ is the Euclidean distance of two words.

For interpretation, we can image that every word has a certain "gravity" to the other words, which is proportional to the square of its local feature scale. If this gravity is larger than a minimal threshold $F_{\min}$, we denote these two words as *GD R-reachable*:

$$F^{i,j} = \varepsilon \frac{\pi(r_i)^2 \pi(r_j)^2}{(R_{i,j})^2}, \qquad \varepsilon \text{ is a constant}$$

$$\tag{5.9}$$

$$F_{i,j} > F_{\min} \rightarrow \varepsilon \frac{\pi(r_i)^2 \pi(r_j)^2}{(R_{i,j})^2} > F_{\min} \rightarrow R_{i,j} < Cr_ir_j.$$

Similar to **DCM**, the input of the gravity distance-based mining is all instances of visual words. Each instance contains the following attributes: *original local features*, *visual word ID*, *location*, and *scale* of this local feature (word instance). To unify the description, we embed the *word ID* of each feature with its corresponding *location* into the mining. Then, we run the similar procedure as in **DCM** to mine colocation patterns. Algorithm 5.1 outlines the workflow of our gravity distance-based visual pattern mining. Figure 5.4 shows some case studies of the mined patterns between the gravity-based pattern mining and the Euclidean distance-based pattern mining.

Algorithm 5.1 Gravity distance based visual pattern mining

---

1 **Input**: Visual vocabulary $\mathbf{V}$, reference images $\{I_i\}_{i=1}^{N}$, reference images with respect to the ToI $\{\{I_i^{ToI_t}\}_{i=1}^{n_t}\}_{t=1}^{M}$, bag-of-words histograms $\{\mathbf{V}(1),\ldots\mathbf{V}(N)\}$, support threshold s, confidence threshold γ, maximal pattern order K, sparse factor α.

2 **Output**: CBoP pattern set $\{Q\}_{i=1}^{n_{selected}}$.

3 **3D Sphere Coding**: **for** *the tth ToI* ($t \in [1, M]$) **do**

4   Build the 3D point cloud using structure-from-motion with bundle adjustment;

5   Build transactions $\{\mathbf{D}\}_t$ by 3D sphere coding in the point cloud with *GD R-reachable distance*;

6 **end**

7 Ensemble $\{\mathbf{D}\}_t$ for all ToI ($t \in [1, M]$) as $\mathbf{D} = \{\mathbf{D}\}_{t=1}^{M}$;

8 // **Gravity Distance based Pattern Mining**

9 Calculate itemset supports and confidences by Equation (5.3), (5.4);

10 Filtering out unreliable pattern candidates with thresholds s and γ;

11 Ouput patterns $\mathbf{P} = \{\mathbf{P}_t\}_{t=1}^{M}$ by Equation (5.8), (5.7);

12 // **Sparse Pattern Coding**

13 Learn the coding vector $\mathbf{w}$ from $\mathbf{P}$ by Equation (5.10), (5.13).

14 **if** $\{L_i\}_{i=1}^{N}$ *are also available* **then**

15   Conduct supervised coding by Equation (5.12).

16 **end**

Figure 5.4 Case study of the mined patterns between the gravity-based pattern mining and the Euclidean distance-based pattern mining.

5.2.2 Sparse Pattern Coding

Sparse coding formulation. Given the mined pattern collection **P**, not all patterns are equivalently important and discriminative in terms of feature representation. Indeed, there are typically redundancy and noise in this initial pattern mining results. However, how to come up with a compact yet discriminative pattern-level features are left unexploited in the literature. In this section, we formulate the pattern-level representation as a sparse pattern coding problem, aiming to maximally reconstruct the original bag-of-words histogram using a minimal number of patterns.

Formally speaking, let $\mathbf{P} = \{P_1, \ldots, P_L\}$ be the mined patterns with maximal order K. In online coding, given the bag-of-words histogram $\mathbf{V}(q) = [V_1(q), \ldots, V_m(q)]$ extracted from image I_q, we aim to encode $\mathbf{V}(q)$ by using a compact yet discriminative subset of patterns, say $\mathbf{P}(q) \subset \mathbf{P}$. We formulate this target as seeking an optimal tradeoff between the maximal reconstruction capability and the minimal coding length:

$$\arg\min_{\mathbf{w}} \sum_{i=1}^{N} ||\mathbf{V}(i) - \mathbf{w}^T\mathbf{P}(i)||_2 + \alpha||\mathbf{w}||_1, \qquad (5.10)$$

where **P** is the patterns mined previously, from which a minimal set is selected to lossy reconstruct each bag-of-words histogram $\mathbf{V}(i)$ as close as possible. **w** serves as a weighted linear combination of all nonzero patterns in **P**, which pools patterns to encode each $\mathbf{V}(i)$ as:

$$f_{\mathbf{P}}(i) = w_1P_1 + w_2P_2 +, \cdots, w_mP_m, \qquad (5.11)$$

where $[w_1, , w_m]$ is the weighted vector learned to reconstruct $\mathbf{V}(i)$ in Equation (5.10). Each w_j is assigned either 0 or 1, performing a binary pattern selection.

Learning with respect to Equations (5.10) and (5.13) are achieved by spare coding over the pattern pool **P**. While guaranteeing the real sparsity through $\mathcal{L}_0$ is intractable, we approximate a sparse solution for the coefficients **w** using $\mathcal{L}_1$ penalty, which results in a Lasso-based effective solution [124].

Finally, we denote the selected pattern subset as $\mathbf{Q}_{\text{selected}}$, which contains n_{selected} patterns as $[Q_1, \ldots, Q_{n_{\text{selected}}}]$. n_{selected} is typically very small, say 100. Therefore, each reference or query image is represented as an n_{selected}-bin pattern histogram.

Supervised coding. Once the supervised labels $\{L_i\}_{i=1}^{N}$ (e.g., category label or prediction from a compensative source) for reference image $\{I_i\}_{i=1}^{N}$ are also available, we can further incorporate L_i to refine the coding of Equation (5.10) as:

$$\arg\min_{\mathbf{w}} \sum_{i=1}^{N} ||\mathbf{V}(i) - (\mathbf{w}^T\mathbf{u})^T\mathbf{P}(i)||_2 + \alpha||\mathbf{w}||_1, \qquad (5.12)$$

where we integrate the supervised label $\{L_i\}_{i=1}^{N}$ into the coding function of $\mathbf{P}$ for $I(i)$ as:

$$(\mathbf{w}^T\mathbf{u})^T\mathbf{P}(i) = w_1 u_1 P_1 + w_2 u_2 P_2 +, \cdots, w_m u_m P_m. \qquad (5.13)$$

$[u_1, \ldots, u_m]$ adds the prior distribution of patterns to bias the selection of $[w_1, \ldots, w_m]$, where u_j is the discriminability of the jth pattern based on its information gain to L_i:

$$u_j = H(L_i) - H(L_i|P_j) \qquad (5.14)$$

Here, $H(L_i)$ is the prior of label L_i given I_i, $H(L_i|P_j)$ is the conditional entropy of label L_i given P_j, which is obtained by averaging the intraclass observation of P_j divided by the interclass distribution of P_j:

$$H(L_i|P_j) = \frac{p(P_j|L_j)}{\sum_l p(P_j|L_l)}. \qquad (5.15)$$

In this sense, the definition of supervised label L_i is quite flexible, e.g., category labels or positive/negative tags, which also allows the case of missing labels.

In terms of compact visual descriptor, CBoP preserves the higher order statistics comparing to the transitional nonzero coding scheme [112] as well as the state-of-the-art boosting-based codeword selection scheme [120]. Different from all previous unsupervised descriptor learning schemes [69–72, 112], CBoP further provides a supervised coding alternative as an optional choice, which yet differs from the work in [120] that demands online side information from the query.

5.3 CBoP FOR LOW BIT RATE MOBILE VISUAL SEARCH

We demonstrate the advances of the proposed CBoP descriptor in the emerging low bit rate mobile visual search scenario, with application to a large-scale mobile landmark search prototype. In such a scenario, different from sending the query image to cost a large query delivery latency, compact descriptors are directly extracted and sent from the mobile end. Such descriptor(s) is expected to be compact, discriminative, and meanwhile efficient for extraction, so as to reduce the overall query delivery latency.

Search pipeline: Figure 5.5 shows the workflow of using our CBoP descriptor in this prototype: The algorithm extracts local features from the query image, quantize them into a bag-of-words histogram, scan 2D spatial nearby words into potential patterns, and encode the discovered patterns into a CBoP descriptor.[5] We further compress this descriptor into a bin occurrence (hit/nonhit) histogram with residual coding.

In the remote server, the decoding procedure is performed: First, a difference decoding is conducted to obtain CBoP histogram, which is then recovered into a bag-of-words histogram by weighted summing up all nonzero patterns using their original word combinations:

$$V(q)_{recovered} = w^T Q = \sum_{i=1}^{n_{selected}} w_i Q_i \qquad (5.16)$$

The decompressed BoW is subsequently sent to the vocabulary tree-based inverted indexing system where the ranking is conducted. Note that the spatial layouts of words can be also sent to do spatial reranking.

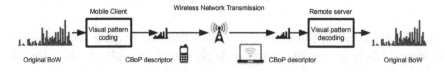

Figure 5.5 The proposed low bit rate mobile visual search framework using CBoP descriptor. Different from previous works in near-duplicate visual search, we emphasize on extremely compact descriptor extraction directly on the mobile end. To achieve zero-latency query delivery, for each query, our CBoP descriptor is typically hundreds of bits. To the best of our knowledge, it is the most compact descriptor with comparable discriminability to the state-of-the-art visual descriptors [16, 112, 113, 125].

---

[5]Note that while the offline patterns are built through 3D sphere coding, in online search we use their 2D codes since we do not have a structure correspondence from the query to the reference point clouds. Not doubt, this would introduce certain distortion, however as shown later in our experiments, superior performance can be still guaranteed.

Efficiency. In our current implementation, given a query image, we only need approximately 2 s to extract the CBoP descriptor. By using techniques such as visual word pruning (e.g., only maintains the visual word centroid features as well as an approximate radius of each word), the storage cost of the vocabulary tree is also very limited.

Contextual learning: There is cheaply available side information in the mobile end, such as GPS tags, compass direction, and base station identity tag. Exploiting the above side information with our supervised coding (Section 5.2.2), the extracted CBoP can be further refined, as detailed in the subsequent experiments (Section 5.4).

5.4 QUANTITATIVE RESULTS

5.4.1 Data Collection

PhotoTourism. First, we validate on the image patch correspondence benchmark. It contains over 100,000 image patches with correspondence labels generated from the point clouds of *Trevi Fountain* (Rome), *Notre Dame* (Paris), and *Half Dome* (Yosemite), all of which are produced by the PhotoTourism system [121]. Each patch correspondence consists of a set of local patches, which is obtained by projecting a given 3D point from the point cloud back to multiple reference images and cropping the corresponding salienct regions.[6] Some exemplar patches obtained through the above procedure are shown in Figure 5.6.

10M landmark photos. To validate our CBoP descriptor in the scalable image retrieval application, we have also collected over 10 million geo-tagged photos from both Flickr and Panoramio websites. We crawled photos tagged within five cities, i.e., *Beijing, New York City, Lhasa, Singapore*, and *Florence*. This dataset is named as *10M landmarks*. Some exemplar photos are shown in Figure 5.7.

We use k-means clustering to partition photos of each city into multiple regions based on their geographical tags. For each city, we select the top 30 densest regions as well as 30 random regions. We then ask a group of volunteers to identify one or more dominant landmark views for

---

[6]Since this dataset contains the ground truth patch correspondences as well as the point clouds from [121, 126], we will skip the 3D sphere coding (Section 5.2) in the following quantitative tests.

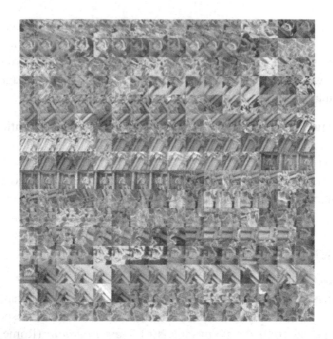

Figure 5.6 Exemplar local patches in the PhotoTourism dataset. Each patch is sampled as 64 × 64 gray scale with a canonical scale and orientation. For details of how the scale and orientation is established, please refer to [126]. These ground truth correspondences are collected from the structure-from-motion-based point cloud construction, with the back projection of the matched points.

Figure 5.7 Exemplar photos collected from Flickr and Panoramio to build our 10M landmarks dataset.

each of these 60 regions. For an identified dominant view, all their near-duplicate photos are manually labeled in its belonged region and nearby regions. Eventually, we have 300 queries as well as their ground truth labels (corrected matched photos) as our test set.

PKUBench. We also evaluate on several typical mobile visual search scenario using *PKUBench*, which is a public available mobile visual search benchmark. This benchmark contains 13,179 scene photos organized into 198 landmark locations, captured by both digital and phone cameras. There are in total 6193 photos captured from digital cameras and 6986 from phone cameras respectively. We recruited 20 volunteers in data acquisition. Each landmark is captured by a pair of volunteers with a portable GPS device (one using digital camera and the other using phone camera). Especially, this benchmark includes four groups of exemplar mobile query scenarios (in total 118 images):

- *Occlusive query set*: 20 mobile queries and 20 corresponding digital camera queries, occluded by foreground cars, people, and buildings.
- *Background cluttered query set*: 20 mobile queries and 20 corresponding digital camera queries, captured far away from a landmark, where GPS search yields worse results due to the signal bias of nearby buildings.
- *Night query set*: 9 mobile phone queries and 9 digital camera queries, where the photo quality heavily depends on the lighting conditions.
- *Blurring and shaking query set*: 20 mobile queries with blurring or shaking and 20 corresponding digital camera queries without any blurring or shaking.

5.4.2 Evaluation Criteria

Effectiveness: We use mean Average Precision (*mAP*) to evaluate our performance, which is also widely used in the state-of-the-art works [24, 27, 30, 113, 125]. *mAP* reveals the position-sensitive ranking precision by the returning list:

$$MAP@N = \frac{1}{N_q} \sum_{i=1}^{N_q} \left(\frac{\sum_{r=1}^{N} P(r)rel(r)}{\min(N, \# - \text{relevant} - \text{images})} \right) \qquad (5.17)$$

where N_q is the number of queries, r is the rank, N is the number of related images for query i, $rel(r)$ is a binary function on the relevance of r, and $P(r)$ is the precision at the cut-off rank of r.

Note that here we have a min operation between the top N returning and #-relevant-images. In a large-scale search system, there are always over hundreds of ground truth relevant images to each query. Therefore, dividing by #-relevant-images would result in a very small MAP. Alternatively, a better choice is the division by the number of returning images. We use min(N, #-relevant-images) to calculate MAP@N.[7]

---

[7]In the case that N is smaller than the number of labeled ground truth, we can simplify min(N, #-relevant-images) with N in subsequent calculation. The min(N, #-relevant-images) operation is a common evaluation in the TRECVID evaluation.

Efficiency: We use the descriptor compactness, i.e., the size of the descriptor stored in the memory or hard disk (for instance 1KB per descriptor etc.).

5.4.3 Baselines

- *Bag-of-words*: Transmitting the entire BoW has the lowest compression rate. However, it provides an mAP upper bound to the other BoW compression strategies.
- *2D patterns*: Instead of obtaining the initial pattern candidates through 3D sphere coding, using the point cloud, we adopt the traditional 2D spatial coding from individual reference images as initially proposed in [72]. This baseline validates the effectiveness of our proposed 3D sphere coding strategy.
- *LDA [115]*: One straightforward alternative in abstracting compact features from the bag-of-words histogram is the topic model features [78, 114, 115]. In this paper, we implement the well-used Latent Direchellet Allocation (LDA)-based feature in [115] as our baseline.
- *CHoG [113]*: We also compare our CBoP descriptor to the CHoG local descriptor, which is a state-of-the-art alternative as introduced in [113].
- *Tree histogram coding [112]*: In terms of image-level compact descriptor, we further implement the tree histogram coding scheme proposed by Chen et al. [112], which is a lossless BoW compression that uses residual coding to compress the BoW histogram.
- *LDVC [120]*: Finally, we compare our CBoP descriptor with the state-of-the-art compact descriptor to the best of our knowledge [120], which adopts location discriminative coding to boost a very compact subset of words. To compare to our unsupervised CBoP, we used reference images from the entire dataset (i.e., landmark photos from the entire city) to train the LDVC descriptor. To compare to our supervised CBoP, we adopt the location label to train a location sensitive descriptor as in [120].

5.4.4 Quantitative Performance

Efficiency analysis. We deploy the low bit rate mobile visual search prototype on HTC Desire G7 as a software application. The HTC DESIRE G7 is equipped with an embedded camera with maximal 2592×1944 resolution, a Qualcomm MSM7201A processor at 528 MHz, a 512M ROM + 576M RAM memory, 8G extended storage and an embedded GPS. Table 5.1 shows the time cost with comparisons to state-of-the-arts in [112, 120, 125]. In our CBoP descriptor extraction, the most time-consuming part is the local

Table 5.1 Time (Second) requirements for CBoP and other alternatives on the mobile end

Compression methods	Local feature(S)	Descriptor coding(S)
BoW histogram	1.25	0.14
Aggregate local descriptors [125]	1.25	164
Tree histogram coding [112]	1.25	0.14
Vocabulary Boosting[120]	1.25	0.14
CBoP		

feature extraction, which can be further accelerated by random sampling, instead of using the interest point detectors [9, 113].

Rate distortion analysis. To compare our CBoP descriptors to the baselines [112, 113, 125], we give the rate distortion analysis in Figure 5.9, where the compression rates correspond to the descriptor lengths of our CBoP descriptor and the alternatives, while the search distortions correspond to the *mAP* drops of different methods, respectively. As shown in Figure 5.9,

Figure 5.8 Example comparisons in the extreme mobile query scenarios including Occlusive query set, Background cluttered query set, Night query set, *and* Blurring and shaking query set *in the* PKUBench *dataset.*

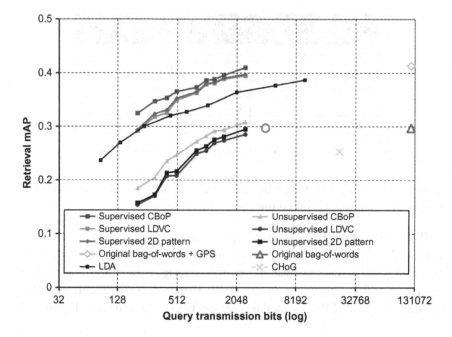

Figure 5.9 Compression rate and ranking distortion analysis with comparison to [112, 113, 125] using the ground truth query set.

our CBoP descriptor has achieved the best tradeoff in the rate distortion evaluation. It reports the highest compression rate with a comparable distortion (by viewing Figure 5.9 horizontally), as well as the highest ranking performance with a comparable compression rate (by viewing Figure 5.9 vertically). In addition, without supervised learning, our CBoP descriptor can still achieve better performance comparing to all alternatives and state-of-the-arts [112, 113, 125]. Figure 5.8 shows some examples in the extreme mobile query scenarios for more intuitive understanding.

5.5 CONCLUSION

In this chapter, we propose to mine discriminative visual patterns from 3D point clouds, based on which learn a CBoP descriptor. Our motivations are twofold: On one hand, while the visual patterns can offer a higher-level abstraction of the bag-of-words representation, the existing mining schemes are misled by the ill-posed pattern configurations from the 2D photographic statistics of individual images. On the other hand, the existing pattern-level representation lacks the capability to offer a compact yet discriminative visual representation, which in turn is crucial for many emerging applications such as low bit rate mobile visual search.

The proposed CBoP descriptor addresses both issues in a principled way: To build a more precise pattern configurations in the real world, we propose to reconstruct 3D point clouds of the target by using structure-from-motion with bundle adjustment, based on which adopt a 3D sphere coding to precisely capture the colocation statistics among words in 3D. To mine more discriminative patterns, a gravity-based distance is introduced into our colocation pattern mining, which embeds the word discriminability into their spatial distances to highlight patterns that contains more discriminative words. Based upon the mined pattern, we further propose to build a compact yet discriminative image representation at the pattern level, named CBoP. CBoP adopts a sparse pattern coding to pursuit a maximal reconstruction of the original bag-of-words histograms with a minimal pattern coding length. Finally, supervised labels can be further incorporated to improve the discriminability of CBoP descriptor.

We have validated the proposed CBoP descriptor in a low bit rate mobile landmark search prototype. We quantitatively demonstrate our advances on both benchmark datasets and a 10-million landmark photo collection. Our CBoP descriptor has shown superior performance over the state-of-the-art pattern mining schemes [72], topic features [115], and compact descriptors [112, 113, 120].

CONCLUSIONS

This book introduced the learning mechanism into the visual local representation and visual dictionary models, aiming to build a more effective computerized visual representation that is more similar to the human visual system. The book began from a learning-based semi-local interest-point detector, with subsequent optimal visual dictionary learning from both unsupervised and supervised perspectives, and ended up exploiting higher-order visual word combinations. During these procedures, the machine-learning mechanism was pervasively embedded into different chapters.

The first contribution of this book was a context-aware semi-local detector (CASL), which emphasized the use of the local interest-point context to build a more semantically and spatially aware semi-local detector, where both spatial context learning and semantic category learning is embedded in the detector construction. The first part of the CASL detector is built over traditional local feature extractions, based on which the spatial context of the local features within the target image is modeled with a multi-scale contextual Gaussian field. Subsequently, a kernalized mean shift procedure is deployed over the contextual field to detect the semi-local features, where the kernel is flexible enough to embed the category information (if available). The relationship between the proposed CASL interest-point detector and the visual saliency model was also revealed and discussed.

The second contribution of this book was an unsupervised way to optimize the visual dictionary, where two main issues were discovered and addressed: (1) The similarity metric bias in hierarchical quantization of local feature space; (2) the lack of adaptive capability for the visual dictionary among different datasets. To address the first issue, a density-based metric learning (DML) was proposed to rectify the biased similarity metric existing in hierarchical k-means clustering. To address the second issue, a vocabulary tree shift approach was presented, which not only addresses the dictionary adaption between different datasets, but also addresses the incremental indexing of dictionary within a dynamically changed dataset.

The third contribution of this book was a generative embedding framework for supervised visual dictionary learning. It proposed adopting the cheaply available, inaccurate Flickr labels to carry supervised dictionary learning, based on the main idea of a hidden Markov random field with the modeling of WordNet-based tag correlation. It was also shown that by simplifying the Markov operations in the proposed model, several widely-used visual dictionary models can be derived from our formulation.

The fourth contribution of this book was to further exploit the higher-order combination of visual words to further improve the effectiveness of visual search and recognition performances. To this end, a gravity-distance based co-location pattern mining approach was proposed, which was shown to outperform the traditional transaction-based co-location pattern mining and distance-based co-location pattern mining. The quantitative experiments also showed its superiority over the existing alternatives.

REFERENCES

[1] H.P. Moravec, Obstacle Avoidance and Navigation in the Real World by a Seeing Robot Rover, Department of Computer Science, Stanford University, 1980.

[2] C. Harris, M. Stephens, A combined corner and edge detector, in: Alvey Vision Conference, vol. 15, Manchester, UK, 1988, p. 50.

[3] K. Rohr, Localization properties of direct corner detectors, J. Math. Imaging Vision 4 (2) (1994) 139–150.

[4] C. Tomasi, T. Kanade, Detection and Tracking of Point Features, Citeseer, 1991.

[5] J. Shi, C. Tomasi, Good features to track, in: IEEE International Conference on Computer Vision and Pattern Recognition, 1994, pp. 593–600.

[6] C.S. Kenney, M. Zuliani, B.S. Manjunath, An axiomatic approach to corner detection, in: IEEE International Conference on Computer Vision and Pattern Recognition, vol. 1, 2005, pp. 191–197.

[7] C. Schmid, R. Mohr, C. Bauckhage, Comparing and evaluating interest points, in: IEEE International Conference on Computer Vision, 1998, pp. 230–235.

[8] D.G. Lowe, Object recognition from local scale-invariant features, in: IEEE International Conference on Computer Vision, Corfu, Greece, 1999, pp. 1150–1157.

[9] D.G. Lowe, Distinctive image features form scale-invariant keypoints, Int. J. Comput. Vision 20 (2) (2004) 91–110.

[10] K. Mikolajczyk, C. Schmid, A performance evaluation of local descriptors, IEEE Trans. Pattern Anal. Mach. Intell. 27 (10) (2005) 1615–1630.

[11] D.H. Hubel, T.N. Wiesel, Receptive fields, binocular interaction and functional architecture in the cat's visual cortex, J. Physiol. 160 (1) (1962) 106–154.

[12] D. Marr, Vision: A Computational Investigation into the Human Representation and Processing of Visual Information, Henry Holt and Co., Inc., New York, NY, USA, 1982.

[13] S.C. Zhu, Y.N. Wu, D. Mumford, Minimax entropy principle and its application to texture modeling, Neural Comput. 9 (8) (1997) 1627–1660.

[14] T. Poggio, F. Girosi, Networks for approximation and learning, Proc. IEEE 78 (9) (2002) 1481–1497.

[15] F.-F. Li, P. Pietro, A Bayesian hierarchical model for learning natural scene categories, in: IEEE International Conference on Computer Vision, Rio de Janeiro, Brazil, 2007.

[16] D. Nister, H. Stewenius, Scalable recognition with a vocabulary tree, in: IEEE International Conference on Computer Vision and Pattern Recognition, New York, USA, 2006.

[17] X. Xie, L. Lu, M. Jia, H. Li, F. Seide, W.-Y. Ma, Mobile search with multimodal queries, Proc. IEEE 4 (2008) 589–601.

[18] Y. Ke, R. Sukthankar, PCA-SIFT: a more distinctive representation for local image descriptors, in: IEEE International Conference on Computer Vision and Pattern Recognition, Washington, DC, USA, 2004, pp. 506–513.

[19] S. Belongie, J. Malik, J. Puzicha, Shape matching and object recognition using shape contexts, IEEE Trans. Pattern Anal. Mach. Intell. 24 (4) (2002) 509–522.

[20] S. Lazebnik, J. Ponce, A sparse texture representation using local affine regions, IEEE Trans. Pattern Anal. Mach. Intell. 27 (8) (2005) 1265–1278.

[21] M. Brown, R. Szeliski, S. Winder, Multi-image matching using multi-scale oriented patches, in: IEEE International Conference on Computer Vision and Pattern Recognition, San Diego, USA, 2005, pp. 510–517.

[22] A. Simon, J. Winder, Learning local image descriptors, in: IEEE International Conference on Computer Vision and Pattern Recognition, Minneapolis, USA, 2007.

[23] G. Hua, M. Brown, S. Winder, Discriminant embedding for local image descriptors, in: IEEE International Conference on Computer Vision, Rio de Janeiro, Brazil, 2007.

[24] J. Philbin, O. Chum, M. Isard, J. Sivic, A. Zisserman, Object retrieval with large vocabularies and fast spatial matching, in: IEEE International Conference on Computer Vision and Pattern Recognition, Minneapolis, USA, 2007.

[25] P. Indyk, N. Thaper, Fast image retrieval via embeddings, in: In 3rd International Workshop on Statistical and Computational Theories of Vision, Nice, France, 2003, pp. 1–15.

[26] H. Jegou, M. Douze, C. Schmid, Hamming embedding and weak geometric consistency for large scale image search, in: European Conference on Computer Vision, Marseille, France, Springer, 2008, pp. 304–317.

[27] G. Schindler, M. Brown, City-scale location recognition, in: IEEE International Conference on Computer Vision and Pattern Recognition, Minneapolis, USA, 2007.

[28] G. Salton, C. Buckley, Term-Weighting Approaches in Automatic Text Retrieval, Morgan Kaufmann Publishers, Inc., San Francisco, USA, 1988.

[29] J. Matas, O. Chum, M. Urban, T. Pajdla, Robust wide-baseline stereo from maximally stable extremal regions, Image Vision Comput. 22 (10) (2004) 761–767.

[30] J. Sivic, J. Philipin, A. Zisserman, Video Google: a text retrieval approach to object matching in videos, in: IEEE International Conference on Computer Vision, Nice, France, 2003, pp. 1470–1477.

[31] F. Jurie, B. Triggs, Creating efficient codebooks for visual recognition, in: IEEE International Conference on Computer Vision, Beijing, China, 2005, pp. 604–610.

[32] J. Yang, Y. Jiang, A.G. Hauptmann, C.-W. Ngo, Evaluating bag-of-visual-words representations in scene classification, in: ACM Multimedia Information Retrieval Conference, Augsburg, Germany, 2007, pp. 197–206.

[33] L. Wang, Toward a discriminative codebook: codeword selection across multi-resolution, in: IEEE International Conference on Computer Vision and Pattern Recognition, Minneapolis, USA, 2007.

[34] T. Leung, J. Malik, Representing and recognizing the visual appearance of materials using 3-D textons, Int. J. Comput. Vis. 43 (1) (2001) 29–44.

[35] H. Jegou, H. Harzallah, C. Schmid, A contextual dissimilarity measure for accurate and efficient image search, in: IEEE International Conference on Computer Vision and Pattern Recognition, Minneapolis, USA, 2007.

[36] D. MacQueen, Information Theory, Inference and Learning Algorithms, Cambridge Press, Cambridge, United Kingdom, 2003.

[37] D. Comaniciu, P. Meer, Mean Shift: a robust approach toward feature space analysis, IEEE Trans. Pattern Anal. Mach. Intell. 24 (5) (2002) 603–619.

[38] S. Basu, M. Bilenko, R.J. Mooney, A probabilistic framework for semi-supervised clustering, in: ACM Conference on Knowledge and Data Discovery, Seattle, USA, 2004, pp. 59–68.

[39] J. Mairal, F. Bach, J. Ponce, G. Sapiro, A. Zisserman, Supervised dictionary learning, in: Advances in Neural Information Processing Systems, Vancouver, Canada, Neural Information Processing Systems Foundation, 2007, pp. 481–488.

[40] S. Lazebnik, M. Raginsky, Supervised learning of quantizer codebooks by information loss minimization, IEEE Trans. Pattern Anal. Mach. Intell. 31 (7) (2009) 1294–1309.

[41] F. Moosmann, B. Triggs, F. Jurie, Fast discriminative visual codebooks using randomized clustering forests, in: Advances in Neural Information Processing Systems, Vancouver, Canada, Neural Information Processing Systems Foundation, 2006, pp. 481–488.

[42] F. Perronnin, C. Dance, G. Csurka, M. Bressan, Adapted vocabularies for generic visual categorization, in: European Conference on Computer Vision, Graz, Austria, Springer, 2006, pp. 464–475.

[43] J. Zhang, M. Marszalek, S. Lazebnik, C. Schmid, Local features and kernels for classification of texture and object categories: a comprehensive review, Int. J. Comput. Vision 73 (2) (2007) 213–238.

[44] J. Liu, Y. Yang, M. Shah, Learning semantic visual vocabularies using diffusion distance, in: IEEE International Conference on Computer Vision and Pattern Recognition, Miami, USA, 2009.

[45] T. Kohonen, Learning vector quantization for pattern recognition, Technical Report, TKK-F-A601, Helsinki Institute of Technology, 1996.

[46] T. Kohonen, Self-Organizing Maps, third ed., Springer, Cambridge, United Kingdom, 2000.

[47] A. Rao, D. Miller, K. Rose, A. Gersho, A generalized VQ method for combined compression and estimation, in: IEEE International Conference on Acoustics, Speech and Signal Processing, Toulouse, France, 1996, pp. 2032–2035.

[48] B. Leibe, A. Leonardis, B. Schiele, Combined object categorization and segmentation with an implicit shape model, in: European Conference on Computer Vision, Prague, Czech, Springer, 2004, pp. 17–23.

[49] S. Agarwal, D. Roth, Learning a sparse representation for object detection, in: European Conference on Computer Vision, Prague, Czech, Springer, 2002, pp. 97–101.

[50] A. Bosch, A. Zisserman, X. Munoz, Scene classification using a hybrid generative/discriminative approach, IEEE Trans. Pattern Anal. Mach. Intell. 30 (4) (2008) 712–727.

[51] A. Gionis, P. Indyk, R. Motwani, Similarity search in high dimensions via hashing, in: International Conference on Very Large Data Bases, Edinburgh, Scotland, Morgan Kaufmann, 1999, pp. 518–529.

[52] G. Shakhnarovich, T. Darrell, P. Indyk, Nearest-Neighbor Methods in Learning and Vision: Theory and Practice, MIT Press, Cambridge, Massachusetts, 2006.

[53] G. Shakhnarovich, P. Viola, T. Darrell, Fast pose estimation with parameter-sensitive hashing, in: International Conference on Computer Vision, Nice, France, 2003, pp. 750–757.

[54] A. Torralba, Y. Weiss, R. Fergus, Small codes and large databases of images for object recognition, in: IEEE Computer Society Conference on Computer Vision and Pattern Recognition, Anchorage, United States, 2008.

[55] Y. Weiss, A. Torralba, R. Fergus, Spectral hashing, in: Advances in Neural Information Processing Systems, Vancouver, Canada, MIT Press, 2008.

[56] B. Kulis, K. Grauman, Kernelized locality-sensitive hashing for scalable image search, in: IEEE International Conference on Computer Vision, Kyoto, Japan, 2009.

[57] M. Raginsky, S. Lazebnik, Locality-sensitive binary codes from shift-invariant kernels, in: Advances in Neural Information Processing Systems, Vancouver, Canada, MIT Press, 2009.

[58] J. Beis, D. Lowe, Indexing without invariants in 3D object recognition, IEEE Trans. Pattern Anal. Mach. Intell. 21 (10) (1999) 1000–1015.

[59] S. Arya, D. Mount, N. Netanyahu, R. Silverman, A. Wu, An optimal algorithm for approximate nearest neighbor searching in fixed dimensions, J. ACM 45 (6) (1998) 891–923.

[60] L. Liang, C. Liu, Y Xu, B. Guo, H. Shum, Real-time texture synthesis by patch-based sampling, ACM Trans. Graph. 20 (3) (2001) 127–150.

[61] G. Hjaltason, H. Samet, Index-driven similarity search in metric spaces, ACM Trans. Database Syst. 28 (4) (2003) 517–580.

[62] S. Nene, S. Nayar, A simple algorithm for nearest neighbor search in high dimensions, IEEE Trans. Pattern Anal. Mach. Intell. 19 (9) (1997) 989–1003.

[63] K. Grauman, T. Darrell, Approximate correspondences in high dimensions, in: Advances in Neural Information Processing Systems, Vancouver, Canada, Neural Information Processing Systems Foundation, 2007, pp. 481–488.

[64] M. Muja, D. Lowe, Fast approximate nearest neighbors with automatic algorithm configuration, in: IEEE International Conference on Computer Vision Theory and Applications, Lisbon, Portugal, 2009.

[65] H. Bay, T. Tuytelaars, L.V. Gool, SURF: speeded up robust features, in: European Conference on Computer Vision, Graz, Austria, Springer, 2006, pp. 404–417.

[66] G. Csurka, C. Bray, C. Dance, L. Fan, Visual categorization with bags of keypoints, in: European Conference on Computer Vision, Workshop on Statistical Learning in Computer Vision, Prague, Czech, Springer, 2004, pp. 1–22.

[67] R. Fergus, P. Perona, A. Zisserman, Object class recognition by unsupervised scale-invariant learning, in: IEEE International Conference on Computer Vision and Pattern Recognition, Madison, USA, 2003, pp. 264–271.

[68] D. Crandall, P. Felzenszwalb, D. Hutternlocher, Spatial priors for part-based recognition using statistical models, in: IEEE International Conference on Computer Vision and Pattern Recognition, San Diego, USA, 2005, pp. 10–17.

[69] J. Sivic, A. Zisserman, Video data mining using configurations of viewpoint invariant regions, in: IEEE International Conference on Computer Vision and Pattern Recognition, Washington, DC, USA, 2004, pp. 488–495.

[70] T. Quack, V. Ferrari, L.V. Gool, Video mining with frequent item set configurations, in: International Conference on Content-Based Image and Video Retrieval, Tempe, USA, Springer, 2006, pp. 360–369.

[71] J. Yuan, Y. Wu, M. Yang, Discovery of collocation patterns: from visual words to phrase, in: IEEE International Conference on Computer Vision and Pattern Recognition, Minneapolis, USA, 2007.

[72] T. Quack, V. Ferrari, L.V. Gool, Efficient mining of frequent and distinctive feature configurations, in: IEEE International Conference on Computer Vision, Rio de Janeiro, Brazil, 2007.

[73] M.A. Fischler, R.C. Bolles, Random sample consensus: a paradigm for model fitting with applications to image analysis and automated cartography, Commun. ACM 24 (1981) 381–395.

[74] T. Li, T. Mei, I.-S. Kweon, X.-S. Hua. Contextual bag-of-words for visual categorization, IEEE Trans. Circuits Syst. Video Technol. 21 (4) (2011) 381–392.

[75] Z. Wu, Q. Ke, M. Isard, J. Sun, Bundling features for large scale partial-duplicate web image search, in: IEEE International Conference on Computer Vision and Pattern Recognition, Miami, United States, 2009.

[76] S. Brin, L. Page. The anatomy of a large-scale hypertextual (web) search engine, in: International World Wide Web Conference, 1998.

[77] T. Hofmann, Probabilistic latent semantic indexing, in: ACM International Conference on Information Retrieval, 1999, pp. 50-57.

[78] D. Blei, A.Y. Ng, M. Jordan, Latent dirichlet allocation, J. Mach. Learn. Res. 3 (2003) 993–1022.

[79] C. Harris, M. Stephens, A combined corner and edge detector, in: Alvey Vision Conference, Haifa, Israel, Alvey Publisher, 1988, pp. 147–152.

[80] K. Mikolajczyk, C. Schmid, Indexing based on scale invariant interest points, in: IEEE International Conference on Computer Vision, Vancouver, Canada, 2001, pp. 525–531.

[81] K. Mikolajczyk, C. Schmid, Scale and affine invariant interest point detectors, Int. J. Comput. Vision 60 (1) (2004) 63–86.

[82] D. Hubel, Eye, Brain and Vision, Scientific American Library, New York, 1995.

[83] M. Gazzaniga, R. Ivry, G. Mangun. Cognitive Neuroscience: The Biology of the Mind, second ed., W.W. Norton, New York, 2002.

[84] P. Viola, M. Jones, Rapid object detection using a boosted cascade of simple features, in: IEEE International Conference on Computer Vision and Pattern Recognition, Hawaii, USA, 2001, pp. 511–518.

[85] H. Lin, J. Si, G.P. Abousleman, Dynamic point selection in image mosaicking, Opt. Eng. 45 (3) (2006) 030501-2–030501-3.

[86] L. Paletta, G. Fritz, C. Seifert, Q-learning of sequential attention for visual object recognition from informative local descriptors, in: International Conference on Machine Learning, Bonn, Germany, International Machine Learning Society, 2005, pp. 649–656.

[87] S. Lazebnik, C. Schmid, J. Ponce, Semi-local affine parts for object recognition, in: Britism Machine Vision Conference, London, United Kingdom, Britism Machine Vision Society, 2004, pp. 959–968.

[88] A. Bruckstein, E. Rivlin, I. Weiss, Scale space semi-local invariants, Image Vision Comput. 15 (5) (1997) 335–344.

[89] S. Bileschi, L. Wolf, Image representations beyond histograms of gradients: the role of gestalt descriptors, in: IEEE International Conference on Computer Vision and Pattern Recognition, Minneapolis, USA, 2007.

[90] A. Torralba, A. Oliva, Contextual guidance of attention in natural scenes: the role of global features on object search, Psychol. Rev. 113 (4) (2006) 766–786.

[91] A. Torralba, K.P. Murphy, W.T. Freeman, Contextual models for object detection using boosted random fields, in: Advances in Neural Information Processing Systems, Vancouver, Canada, Neural Information Processing Systems Foundation, 2004, pp. 1401–1408.

[92] A. Torralba, Contextual priming for object detection, Int. J. Comput. Vision 53 (2) (2003) 169–191.

[93] H. Jegou, C. Schmid, H. Harzallah, J. Verbeek, Accurate image search using the contextual dissimilarity measure, IEEE Trans. Pattern Anal. Mach. Intell. 32 (1) (2009) 2–11.

[94] L. Itti, C. Koch, E. Niebur, A model for saliency-based visual attention for rapid scene analysis, IEEE Trans. Pattern Anal. Mach. Intell. 20 (11) (1998) 1254–1259.

[95] T. Serre, L. Wolf, S. Bileschi, M. Riesenhuber, T. Poggio, Robust object recognition with cortex-like mechanisms, IEEE Trans. Pattern Anal. Mach. Intell. 29 (3) (2006) 411–426.

[96] X. Hou, L. Zhang, Saliency detection: a spectral residual approach, in: IEEE International Conference on Computer Vision and Pattern Recognition, Minneapolis, USA, 2007.

[97] M. Jamieson, S. Dickinson, S. Stevenson, S. Wachsmuth, Using language to drive the perceptual grouping of local image features, in: IEEE International Conference on Computer Vision and Pattern Recognition, New York, USA, 2006.

[98] K. Fukunaga, Statistical Pattern Recognition, second ed., Boston Academic Publishers, Inc., Boston, MA, USA, 1990.

[99] Y. Huang, S. Shekhar, H. Xiong, Discovering collocation patterns from spatial data sets: a general approach, IEEE Trans. Knowl. Data Eng. 16 (12) (2004) 1472–1485.

[100] K. Mikolajczyk, T. Tuytelaars, C. Schmid, A. Zisserman, J. Matas, F. Schaffalitzky, et al. A comparison of affine region detectors, Int. J. Comput. Vision 65 (1-2) (2006) 43–72.

[101] Y. Cheng, Mean shift, model seeking and clustering, IEEE Trans. Pattern Anal. Mach. Intell. 17 (8) (1995) 790–799.

[102] M. Dundar, J. Bi, Joint optimization of cascaded classifiers for computer aided detection, in: IEEE International Conference on Computer Vision and Pattern Recognition, Minneapolis, USA, 2007.

[103] A. Torralba, WordNet Structure in LabelMe, Available from: http://people.csail.mit.edu/torralba/research/LabelMe/wordnet/test.html.

[104] Path Labeling Corespondence Dataset Released in CVPR 2010. Towards semantic embedding in visual vocabulary, Available from: http://vilab.hit.edu.cn/~rrji/index_files/SemanticEmbedding.htm.

[105] C. Fellbaum, WordNet: An Electronic Lexical Database, MIT Press, Massachusetts, USA, 1998.

[106] T. Pedersen, S. Patwardhan, J. Michelizzi, WordNet: similarity-measuring the relatedness of concepts, in: Association for the Advancement of Artificial Intelligence Conference, San Jose, USA, Association for the Advancement of Artificial Intelligence, 2004, pp. 1024–1025.

[107] W. Li, M. Sun, Automatic Image Annotation Based on WordNet and Hierarchical Ensemble, Springer, Computational Linguistics and Intelligent Text Processing, 2006.

[108] S. Geman, D. Geman, Stochastic relaxation, gibbs distributions and the Bayesian restoration of images, IEEE Trans. Pattern Anal. Mach. Intell. 6 (1984) 721–741.

[109] J.M. Hammersley, P. Clifford, Markov fields on finite graphs and lattices, Unpublished manuscript, 1971.

[110] J. Winn, A. Criminisi, T. Minka, Object categorization by learned universal visual dictionary, in: IEEE International Conference on Computer Vision, Beijing, China, 2005.

[111] PASCAL, Pascal voc database, Available from: http://www.PASCAL-network.org/challenges/VOC/.

[112] D. Chen, S. Tsai, V. Chandrasekhar, G. Takacs, J. Singh, and B. Girod. Tree histogram coding for mobile image matching. DCC. 2009.

[113] V. Chandrasekhar, G. Takacs, D. Chen, S, Tsai, R. Grzeszczuk, and B. Girod. CHoG: compressed histogram of gradients a low bit-rate feature descriptor. CVPR. 2009.

[114] F.-F. Li and P. Perona. A Bayesian hierarchical model for learning natural scene categories. CVPR, 2005.

[115] A. Bosch, A. Zisserman, and X. Munoz. Scene classification using a hybrid generative/discriminative approach. PAMI, 2008.

[116] Y. Weiss, A. Torralba, and R. Fergus. Spectral hashing. NIPS, 2008.

[117] T. Hofmann. Unsupervised learning by probabilistic latent semantic analysis. *ML Journal*, 2001.

[118] J. Yang, K. Yu, Y. Gong, and T. Huang. Linear spatial pyramid matching using sparse coding for image classification. *CVPR*, 2009.

[119] R. Fergus, P. Perona, and A. Zisserman. A sparse object category model for efficient learning and exhaustive recognition. *CVPR*, 2005.

[120] R. Ji, L.-Y. Duan, J. Chen, H. Yao, J. Yuan, Y. Rui, and W. Gao. Location discriminative vocabulary coding for mobile landmark search. *IJCV*. 2011.

[121] N. Snavely, S. M. Seitz, and R. Szeliski. PhotoTourism: exploring photo collections in 3D. *SIGGRAPH*, 2006.

[122] R. Agrawal, T. Imielinski, A.N. Swami, Mining association rules between sets of items in large database, in: ACM Conference on Management of Data, Barcelona, Spain, 1993, pp. 207–216.

[123] R. Ji, L.-Y. Duan, J. Chen, and W. Gao. Towards compact topical descriptor. *CVPR*, 2012.

[124] R. Tibshirani. Regression shrinkage and selection via the Lasso. *Journal of the Royal Statistical Society*, 1997.

[125] H. Jegou, M. Douze, C. Schmid, and P. Perez. Aggregating local descriptors into a compact image representation. *CVPR*. 2010.

[126] S. Winder and M. Brown. Learning local image descriptors. *CVPR*, 2007.

[127] G. Salton, A. Wong, C.S. Yang, A vector space model for automatic indexing, Commun. ACM 18 (11) (1975) 613–620.

[128] J. Yang, A. Hauptamann, A text categorization approach to video scene classification using keypoint features, CMU Technical Report, 2006.

[129] M. Mitra, C. Buckley, C. Cardie, A. Singhal, An analysis of statistical and syntactic phrases, in: Recherche d'Information Assistée par Ordinateur, New York, USA, 1997, pp. 200–217.

[130] ETH-Zurich, Zurich building image database, Available from: http://www.vision.ee.ethz.ch/showroom/zubud/index.en.html.

[131] H. Shao, T. Svoboda, V. Ferrari, T. Tuytelaars, L.V. Gool, Fast indexing for image retrieval based on local appearance with re-ranking, in: IEEE International Conference on Image Processing, Barcelona, Spain, 2003, pp. 737–740.

Printed in the United States
By Bookmasters